I0050518

Powerful Performance

Powerful Performance

How to Be Influential, Ethical, and Successful in Business

Mark Eyre

BEP BUSINESS EXPERT PRESS

Powerful Performance: How to Be Influential, Ethical, and Successful in Business
Copyright © Business Expert Press, LLC, 2019.

All rights reserved. No part of this publication may be reproduced, stored in a retrieval system, or transmitted in any form or by any means—electronic, mechanical, photocopy, recording, or any other except for brief quotations, not to exceed 250 words, without the prior permission of the publisher.

First published in 2019 by
Business Expert Press, LLC
222 East 46th Street, New York, NY 10017
www.businessexpertpress.com

ISBN-13: 978-1-94858-002-1 (paperback)
ISBN-13: 978-1-94858-003-8 (e-book)

Business Expert Press Business Ethics and Corporate Citizenship Collection

Collection ISSN: 2333-8806 (print)
Collection ISSN: 2333-8814 (electronic)

Cover and interior design by S4Carlisle Publishing Services Private Ltd., Chennai, India

First edition: 2019

10 9 8 7 6 5 4 3 2 1

Printed in the United States of America.

Abstract

How do you empower yourself to maximize your impact? This book will show you how to do this ethically, using the nine key steps.

- Do you feel that your work and life should somehow be better than it is?
- Are you on a treadmill, doing things you don't want to do, with no hope of getting off?
- Do you find it hard to say what you want or even to know what you want?
- Are you intimidated by those in authority, whoever they are?

If so, then *Powerful Performance* is for you.

Join Mark Eyre on a journey to discover how you can be both ethical and powerful, and that it doesn't have to be a choice between them, in business or in life. Through reading the insights and case studies in this book and completing the self-diagnostic exercises, you will learn the nine steps to ethical power. Mastering these steps will enable you to stand your ground and achieve your full potential.

Keywords

assertive behavior; business ethics; ethical power; influencing; personal development; personal leadership; personal power; self-belief; self-empowerment; self-esteem; self-expression; self-help

Contents

Introduction

The people who are crazy enough to think they can change the world, are the ones who do.

—Rob Siltanen

Life and Power

Cast your mind back to your younger days. Do you remember what it felt like to be a teenager? To go through education? To move into your first job? Have you ever noticed the exuberance of youth? I remember what that was like. In my late teens and early 20s, I felt empowered, as if I could change the world. I could do anything I wanted and be anyone I wanted. There were no constraints; the world was mine. You may have felt like this at some point in your career or life. It's a great feeling.

So, what happened?

Life happened. Life in all its forms. Life, good and bad. If we're lucky, more of it will be good, and if we're unlucky more of it will be bad. But either way, something interesting happens. Isn't it funny how the bad things often weigh far more heavily on us? If somebody criticizes us at work, it leaves a bigger mark than if someone else praises us? A variety of studies have shown that for every bad thing that happens, we need around five good things to happen to offset that.[1] I'll leave it to science to explain why this is, but avoidance of pain is a very big motivator for us human beings. Much of it is instinctive, a desire to avoid danger.

Of course, in precivilized days, danger meant being killed or eaten. Nowadays, danger may mean being verbally attacked by our manager during a presentation we are giving. But the instinctive reaction is the same, if we perceive we're under threat. Bad things happening have a disproportionate effect on us, and they impact on our sense of self and power. The result is we lose those feelings of great power and anticipation of our younger days, if we were lucky enough to have them. What's more, where we have been burned before (by specific situations or specific people), we will be much warier next time. This wariness reduces our sense of power.

As we mature, events can grind us down. This book is about learning to reclaim our power.

The Context to Power

Power is all around us. We live in families and communities. We work in organizations and have relationships with suppliers, customers, and other stakeholders. We are educated in schools, colleges, and universities. We are members of professional associations. Perhaps we go to church, and we may be members of a wide range of social organizations. Why, even if we live home alone, we are increasingly subject to the virtual world of social networking, with its own set of rules and ways of doing things. We all have friends and networks. We are all members of society and deal with authority in its different guises: tax authorities, police, traffic wardens, and inspectors of many types. Unless we've won the lottery, we are financially dependent on others. In other words, power is important. How we deal with this is central to what we get out of our work and life.

But there's a twist to this tale. We are increasingly surrounded by a very different language, particularly in Western societies and our business organizations. It is the language of empowerment, democracy, participation, consultation, and involvement. All *nice* language, but it carries a seed that causes a great many people to become power ill.

So, what is this virus that can cause a power illness? It's the virus of invisibility. Power is often more masked, cloaked, and less visible than before. *Nice* words often mask where power really lies, making it more possible to be oblivious to it.

Sixty years ago, society was organized in a very clear way. We were born (predominantly) into two-parent families and woe betides us if we stepped out of line. Schools were strict and the workplace largely a place of fear with their attendant command-and-control cultures. Religion held a much stronger hold over people; what was said in the pulpit was literally gospel. Upper, middle, or working class, everyone knew their place.

What was clear in those days was who held the power over you and where they held it. In other words, you knew where you had no rights, even though it might have felt unjust. But consider what it's like now, as we approach the end of the second decade of this millennium.

Nowadays, we might be born into a one- or two-parent family, and it might change during our formative years. Corporal punishment is history in schools. Empowerment and involvement are key buzzwords in workplaces now, and religion is in decline in much of society. It's hard to say what *class* is anymore (even if *rich* and *poor* are obvious). We have never had access to so much information, as opposed to being kept in the dark. So, are we more empowered, and more able to control our lives than before?

Yes, to a degree, although economic advancement may be more the reason for this than anything else. However, when I watch the wars abroad, the recent global recession, the conduct of the banks preceding the banking collapse, the greed in the global stock markets, and the behavior of business leaders, it is hard to feel empowered. I know I am not the only person who feels this.

The danger that lurks in modern life is that power is much less clear, less visible, and less obvious in all walks of life. Instead, power is deployed subtly. This means that unless we are alert and vigilant, we may become disempowered without even knowing it. For one example of this, look no further than the literature on work–life balance. This debate is disguised as an issue of choice. But I have rarely met anyone who wants to have more work and less life! It's usually the other way around. We work because we need to earn money to live, and companies and work organizations want as many hours out of us as they can get. One way to do this without demanding it is to establish informal rules about when people leave the office and pile the work on to make it harder to leave. After all, you can't leave until you've finished your work, just as a child isn't allowed to leave the dinner table before he or she has finished their meal. Then there's the laptop, tablet, and smartphone, all presented as technology that frees us up. Yet many people now feel as if they are chained to these gadgets.

It's very easy to become disempowered nowadays. I've met hundreds if not thousands of people personally who feel disempowered, disengaged, and disillusioned. Even outward appearances of success cannot disguise this inward sense that our life is not our own.

What Is Ethical Power?

Let's start by giving some idea of what ethical power is and what it isn't. Defining it matters because, as we will go on to see, many people see *power* as a dirty word.

Ethical power is about making sure our needs and wants are pursued, but in such a way that we don't trample upon the needs and wants of other people along the way. Ethical power recognizes that we're here to live a real life, to achieve real things, to engage and develop our talents, and to be who we want to be. Ethical power is essential to long-term business success.

With ethical power, you believe you have the right to be powerful. No one has the right to tell you how to live your life. Equally, you do not have the right to tell others how to live theirs. Ethical power also means we must be ready to take the consequences of our decisions and behavior. It does not hide behind other people, including decision by committee even where some decisions may be taken that way.

The nine steps to ethical power outlined in this book show us how we can be both powerful and ethical. It means we can live and work in our own way, which is ultimately what most of us want.

The relationship between power and ethics is a key issue for our time. Our dilemma is that we cannot rely on other people to deliver it. Ethical power begins at home, and that means translating its principles into our own work, homes, and lives. It is for each of us to step up to the plate.

Why Does It Matter?

As a trainer, personal developer, and coach, I have met many people from all walks of life, including young people, the middle-aged, people near the end of their working life, and even pensioners—from senior managers and executives through to people going through redundancy or those grappling with the implications of change or facing outside life challenges. The key theme that emerges again and again is how to exercise power ethically so that we can influence what goes on and without undermining other people around us. My work has largely been concerned with empowering people to make decisions and get on with their lives, usually in a working context.

During the last 25 years, I have encountered many people who have had a significant issue with holding their own personal power. This has included difficulties with being assertive through to being on a career path they fundamentally did not want to be on, facing tough domestic circumstances or workplace bullying. The nature of my help has varied during my career from a more practical helping approach in the human resource roles I've been in to a personal development or coaching approach.

The Power Formula

This book is divided into three main sections, which correspond to the different elements of the power formula: *Power = energy × application*.

We need to have energy if we are to be powerful. It's obvious that no energy results in no power. But it is equally important that we learn to apply our energy in real situations. Otherwise, again, we aren't powerful.

Part 1 of this book looks at the power part of this equation, becoming familiar with different aspects of what power is, both in theory and, more importantly, in your own practice. Starting to recognize the different aspects to power, and how you're dealing with each of them, is important.

In Part 2, I emphasize the part of the equation that deals with energy. Finding ways to raise our own energy level is critical. Take one look at a disempowered person, and what do you see? Often, what you see is a listless person, going nowhere careerwise, and not having much energy to do or talk about anything. This is no formula for a productive, happy life.

Part 3 of the book focuses on the importance of applying your power in an ethical way. That way, not only do you benefit from this, but so do the people around you, including those who are most important in your life.

There are exercises in each chapter, designed to enable you to apply the nine steps to ethical power. One key to becoming a more empowered individual is to act, so I would strongly encourage you to complete these exercises.

Power and Personal Development

There is much self-help literature already out there on finding your purpose, working out your personal values, becoming more assertive, looking at psychology, positive thinking, and challenging your own personal limitations and beliefs. Yet, in my work, I see many unhappy people who are well read in this area. They seem unable to make the changes they want to make. Many of them seem clear on the following things:

- They know what changes they would like to make in an ideal world.
- They are discontented with their present position.
- They have some idea of what they want to do and what sort of person they want to be.

So why doesn't the desired change happen?

The central argument in this book is that the biggest single thing that holds people back is that we fail to deal with the issue of our own power. Part of the reason for this may be that *power* is seen as a dirty word and therefore to be avoided at all costs. The media is full of stories about abuse of power, from political leaders to teachers, social workers, priests, executive directors, and bankers. The list is endless. Who would want to abuse power in this way? Those whom we see as powerful are often abused by the public in turn, so who would want power? And yet some people clearly are attracted to power. It is seductive, impressive, and it gives great opportunities to use power for our own ends. Most of us would never do this of course, would we? As a result, we shy away from power, and may not even want to talk about it. That isn't good enough. It is only through mastering the key steps to ethical power that we can genuinely transform our working lives for the better as well as the lives of those around us.

We all have potential to be powerful. However, I believe that many people are genuinely scared of their own potential power and shy away from using it to anything like its maximum effect. As Marianne Williamson said in a quote subsequently widely attributed to Nelson Mandela,

Our deepest fear is not that we are inadequate. Our deepest fear is that we are powerful beyond measure.[2]

She goes on to point out that as we shine our own light more powerfully, the effect is to encourage other people to do the same thing. In other words, empowerment breeds empowerment.

There are many reasons why we end up fearing taking our own power, and this book will examine them. More importantly, we will look at your own power positions and how to exercise your power in a constructive way to get more out of your career and life.

Taking Up Ethical Power

I hope you enjoy reading this book, and that it gives you plenty of food for thought. The ability to be heard, and to influence events and people around us, is critical if our life is to have meaning. Our ability to make choices and decisions is inhibited without ethical power. As we will see, power and energy are closely linked; when we feel empowered, we also feel energized, and vice versa. If you want to move into much closer alignment with the kind of life you have always wanted to live, achieve your work goals, and become a better person in the process, then ethical power is for you.

You have choices to make. You can choose to make them. Enjoy the ride. As I mentioned earlier, life is for living. So, stand up for yourself and start living your life.

Mark Eyre
September 17, 2018

PART 1

The Concept of Power

CHAPTER 1

Power Scenarios

There are two types of people who will tell you that you cannot make a difference in this world: those who are afraid to try and those who are afraid you will succeed.

—Ray Goforth

The purpose of this chapter is to highlight some lessons about power that might encourage you to examine what happens to you. Outlined below are some cameos of power in modern life; you may want to put yourself in the position of the people in them. You might even recognize some of them from your own experience. All of these are based on my work with coaching clients in the last decade or so—managers, executives, and staff.

Thought for the Day

I turn my mind off, not daring to think about my day as I walk in for a project team meeting. A scene like this is enacted every week, and it is one that I dread. It is a 2-hour business meeting with associates I don't want to see, a manager I don't want to hear, and a project I don't want to be involved in. It's funny how I always end up with most of the work. No doubt, today I'd be asked to account for what I'd done since last week's meeting. If previous experience is anything to go by, it will feel like a trial, and I will be corrected in public for everything that isn't completed to everyone else's satisfaction.

Then there's my team meeting this afternoon. A less responsible, disempowered bunch of losers it's hard to imagine. They won't do anything off their own back without consulting me in triplicate. No wonder I never get around to doing my own job. With any luck, they'll make me redundant one day soon. Then I can go abroad for 6 months and think about what I really want to do.

At least tomorrow, I can go to the football with my mates, have a few drinks, and if my team win, that will make up for this week and make it all worthwhile.

The Dictatorial Boss

I must have looked like a man who'd been given the choice of which animal to kill first with his bare hands: a lion or a tiger. My memories of what now felt like an idyllic time on a riverboat at the weekend were long gone. The recession of my idyllic memories accelerated on receipt of a cordial invitation from Jane's personal assistant to see Jane at 2 o'clock. That meant one of the following:

1. Some work was coming my way,
2. She wants to tell me what one of my team members did while I was away (usually not good), or
3. She wants to know how last week's conference went.

I hoped it wasn't number three. Although I'd started working on my conference report, in no way could it be described as *finished* (though that might soon become a great description for me). For one thing, I hadn't physically completed the first draft. Secondly, with last week's events and my domestic crisis, my brain was not operating anywhere near its optimal analytical peak. In other words, my first draft was crap. But even if it was a brilliant and completed version, Jane would have expected a final version on her desk by now.

This left me an hour to complete something to take in with me, having forfeited my lunch break. Good thing I didn't feel hungry then; even the knots in my stomach were in knots.

Realizing I couldn't get the report completed, I concentrated on tightening up what I'd already written and thinking about the verbal report I could give her. I could at least make that sound convincing. But Jane would ask why it wasn't ready, especially when I'd said nothing to contradict her assumption made before conference week that I would do it at the weekend. I mulled over alternative scenarios about what to say on this, mostly badged with the theme *unexpected weekend event.* The only other option was to go for the *couldn't be bothered* range. But that would be followed by the *near-certain exit* riposte from Jane. Rumor had it that the Hubble telescope had been trained on her once for a week and failed to discover any evidence of a personal life. Unfortunately, she applies the same nonexistent personal life standard to everyone else in the office.

Meanwhile, deep inside me, a voice pointed out all the negative ways I was putting myself down right now and taking my own self-belief away. Jane wouldn't need to do much to smudge me on the floor. I was already smudging myself into oblivion.

∞

Jane's assistant let me in when I called at the appointed time. I was ushered in, the door closed, and the inevitable questions were asked in the right order.

1. How was the conference last week?
2. Have you completed my report?

Fine was as far as I got in summarizing how the conference went, given Jane's open hand, which indicated the lack of a report.

"I wasn't able to complete the report over the weekend." The words were assertive, but I struggled to keep my voice steady.

"You promised me you would have it ready for today."

"I will have it done by the end of today."

"Oh, that's rather disappointing. I promised the director a summary by that time. How do you suggest I do that?"

"I could tell you about it now," I offered helpfully, or as helpfully as I could.

"Looks like that will have to do" was the response. Not pleasant, but not the complete roasting she has been known to dish out.

The meeting settled down from there. I summarized as best I could the key points from the 3 days, with the help of the notes I already had. I promised to have my completed report ready by the end of the day.

Time to exit stage left. At least I was still alive.

How It Feels

My name is James Anderson, and I have this deep sense of unease. Behind it lies the feeling that right now I'm not where I ought to be. I'm not doing what I ought to do. That life is not all it could be.

Every day, I get up, and from that point on I spend a lot of energy getting exactly nowhere. My life is just one long treadmill. Now that wouldn't be bad if the treadmill was going in the direction I wanted to go in. But it's pushing me backward, which means I must run just to stand still. No wonder I feel tired all the time.

I can see my tombstone now, and the epitaph somewhat hauntingly says:

Here lies James Anderson; he never quite knew where he was in life, but he does now!

Failure to Convince a Superior

My name is Alison. I used to work for a charitable organization with an uncharitable director in charge. He was dictatorial and often did not take advice from people who knew more about what was going on. One day, he called me into his office, saying I must arrange for one of his staff, Joe Timson, to be fired. Yet Joe was completely unaware that he wasn't performing well, and indeed his immediate manager had told him at his last appraisal that he was doing quite well.

I advised the director not to take this action, and that if there was an issue with Joe, he should give him a warning instead and a chance to improve. But there was no stopping the director. Joe was fired, unfairly in my opinion.

One year on, with Joe taking legal action against the organization, claiming damages for unfair dismissal, the director in question again called me into his office. Before I'd even had the chance to sit down, he lambasted me for incompetence, alleging that I didn't warn him of the risks of firing Joe. I tried to defend myself, and the conversation went as follows:

Director: This is your fault!
Me: I did say you should give Joe a warning if you had a problem with his performance. I tried to say. . .
Director: It is your fault. You failed to convince me! That makes it your fault!

Parental Approval

"Well, you're on a good career path, aren't you, son, with regular pay rises. You're working for a stable company. You two still have time on your side."

"What about if I'm not happy in that job, for a start?"

"Why, what's wrong with it?"

"I don't enjoy it. I'm asked to do things that are dishonest, unethical. There's nowhere further for me to go there."

"I'm sorry; I don't understand why you want to go anywhere. It's secure. You're well-off."

"Yeah, like I'm in a prison palace."

"What do you want then? It could be worse; you could be in the armed forces."

"Yes, it could be worse. It could also be better. Come on, Mum, you've done work for charity. You know what it is to want to do some good in the world."

"True, Son, but you've got to look after your home base first. I did that when I brought you all up. Your father worked hard to get you where you are now."

"I appreciate that; I really do. But that was your choice. And this is mine."

"What choice are you making son? To destroy a marriage—she's a great woman. To lose your job? Your house? Think what you could lose, Craig, before you go tearing in."

"First of all, I'm not tearing anywhere. Second, I've lost who I am, and I want me back. Third, there are other houses, and big isn't always best."

"We can't believe what we're hearing," and so on. . .

The no-win game. I realized that's where I was. It mattered not a jot what I said. It mattered not how passionately I said it. My parents were so used to prisons that they could not even see what it might be like to be free. They talked like they were only one person for goodness sake—*we can't believe what we're hearing* . . . I want a partner, but I don't want to be joined at the brain with her, putting on some sort of *we're united* show for the benefit of the whole of humankind. Their view might have been OK for their generation—a comfortable prison was better than a lousy one. You had to marry and have kids—you had to conform. There's more choice now, if we decide to choose. I was deciding to, and they didn't have a cat in hell's chance of ever understanding.

"Craig, we just don't understand what's gotten into you."

"Life! That's what's gotten into me. A desire for life."

The Helpless Trap

Some of the above situations will make you smile, while others may appall you. But the one thing they all have in common is that they either deal with people who have already lost much of their power or typify situations that have the impact of undermining people in different ways.

If we allow our power to be undermined, we risk suffering the consequences of living a disempowered, helpless life. We'll end up feeling unhappy about our work, about our life, not feeling like it is our own. Other people may be making the key decisions that affect us, without our having much of a say. We're likely to end up feeling negative and not looking forward to the future. How can we look forward to it when we have little say in what happens? Disempowered people end up losing control over their lives, or large portions thereof. Life becomes a treadmill, a succession of events over which we have no control and little influence. We do indeed risk ending up feeling like we're living someone else's life.

When I was at school, I remember a story about a guy called Martin Buber. It goes something like this: when he died and was admitted to Heaven, he was called to account for himself in his life. One of the questions he was asked was:

> I don't want to know why you weren't Moses or Einstein or Mozart in your life. I just want to know why on earth you weren't Martin Buber?[1]

It sounded like old Martin Buber had sold his life out and lost who he was.

I heard that story when I was a teenager, and I vowed to always be myself and think for myself. That's an aspiration that is easier said than done. This book will set out how we can do it.

Power and Ethics

Given the consequences of disempowerment, you would think more people would choose to pursue the path of power. Yet many choose not to.

There is one obvious reason why this is: the word *power* has a negative connotation. If ever there was a word that needed an image makeover, this is it. *Power* as a word is in trouble! The reason is not hard to find. The following statement is widely supported:

Powerful people have no ethics; ethical people have no power!

This stance has some research to support it in the workplace. Dacher Keltner points out the following in his work, *The power paradox*:

Studies also show that once people assume positions of power, they're likely to act more selfishly, impulsively, and aggressively, and they have a harder time seeing the world from other people's points of view. This presents us with the paradox of power.[2]

Keltner goes on to point out the importance of staying vigilant when we are in a position of power over others.

Many people hold to the belief that we can be powerful or we can be ethical, but we cannot ever be both. Clearly, this is not the case. However, when we look at how power is wielded in society, it's easy to see why many people believe it. We hear of so many abuses of power by those in authority that it becomes hard to equate ethics with power. However, these abuses do not make the above statement true. After all, some of the most widely acknowledged great leaders were very ethical in their approach. People like Mohandas Gandhi, Martin Luther King Junior, and Nelson Mandela held great power but were immensely ethical with it. The activities of philanthropic business leaders down the decades also highlight that power and ethics can go together.

A further imperative for choosing the path of power is that it is essential if we want to fulfill our potential as human beings and succeed in our career. Retaining and enhancing our own power is vital if we want to develop ourselves. Power and personal development go closely together. In the next chapter, we will explore this point in more detail.

CHAPTER 2

The Disempowerment Game

Successful people do what unsuccessful people are not willing to do.
Don't wish it were easier; wish you were better.

—Jim Rohn

If ever you doubted the central importance of power to our own development as human beings, just consider the following example of a working
mindset that I've come across many times:

My work:

I've been a compliance manager in my company for the last
2 years. In my role, I make sure my company complies with all financial services legislation. In a fast-changing industry, I have a satisfying
job, making a major contribution to an organization that provides our
customers with the prosperity and security to achieve all their dreams
in life. My role is the culmination of a purposeful career path that has
taken me through different jobs in the industry, from sales to customer
services and operations. So I have a thorough understanding of the demands faced as we begin to approach the third decade of this century.

Right, enough of this bullshit. I'm even boring myself by telling
you this. Goodness knows how recruitment interviewers must feel
hearing all this stuff day after day. Now, I'll tell you the truth. Deep
down there's something missing in my work. What's missing is the
feeling that I'm doing something genuinely useful in the world. It
doesn't have to be feeding the poor, helping the homeless, or tending
to the sick. Even just doing something that makes a difference to other

(*Continued*)

people would be a step up. I don't feel like I'm making a difference that matters to anyone.

Things haven't always been like this. When I graduated from university 14 years ago, with a second-class degree in English and history, the world looked a far better place. I could do anything I wanted and be whoever I wanted. The world looked exciting. So, what happened?

I'm not sure really. It's as if the fire went out of me. I don't think there was one point where it went, but it probably did over a period of time. The redundancy 5 years ago didn't help. That gave a big knock to my confidence at work, the first time I've failed in my career. I think it was just that my face didn't fit and given the opportunity to get rid of a few people, the powers that be took the chance and removed me.

At that time, I worked in sales. I was lucky enough to get some help with finding a new job, though, and I did all those exercises along the lines of *what work suits you best?* I realized that sales didn't suit me best but maybe something more in people management or compliance would do so. Doing things fairly has always been important to me. I like to think that people should be treated fairly; going into a job that allowed me to do this seemed a good idea. My next job after this was managing a team in an operations environment. This was ironic because one of my first jobs was to make some of my team redundant. I did not enjoy this, and although I tried to be fair, my then boss was heavily involved in the decisions, and I hadn't been around long enough to have the main say. I disagreed with some of his decisions, but I was the one that carried them out.

This was one reason I moved to my current job, to promote fairness in what we sell to customers. But even this leaves me feeling hollow.

Still, in 30 years, I can think about retiring.

Does any of this resonate with you? Do you recognize anyone who feels like this? These feelings are all too common and sum up what it is to fundamentally lose control of your working life. This person has clearly given up any sense of personal responsibility for it, but the personal discontent remains for all to see.

The irony is that if this represents how we feel about work and life (and it does for many people), then the only person out there who can change it is ourselves. Holding our own power is essential to achieve great things in our career and to live the life we want. That makes finding it, and holding on to it, key to developing ourselves and achieving the goals we have. By contrast, the consequences of giving up power are profound and costly in the long term.

There are several reasons why we might disempower ourselves as well as why other people might take our power away from us. We will consider each in turn.

Ways We Disempower Ourselves

We may choose to give up our power to other people, for a range of reasons. Some key reasons are outlined below.

Reason 1: The Comfort Factor

Sometimes, it is comfortable to let others take responsibility, especially where we don't like challenge. Now, I'm not expecting everyone to like to be challenged, or to challenge themselves, all the time. However, if we avoid challenge completely, then we risk always taking the cozy comfort option by letting others make the decisions for us rather than making them ourselves, or at least participating in them. We can even end up becoming apathetic; show me an apathetic person, and I'll show you someone who is disempowered, or someone who disempowered themselves. We risk sacrificing our long-term happiness in pursuit of the easy life in the short term. As the support and challenge model in Figure 2.1 suggests, we need to break out of the cycle of comfort and apathy, instead challenging ourselves to do more, or do better.

This model is derived from Sanford's theory of challenge and support, which was originally focused on student development.[1] However, it can be applied more widely. As the model clearly suggests, we must move toward a situation where we challenge ourselves if we are to achieve high performance in whatever we do. Of equal importance, we need high levels of self-support as well as supportive relationships with other people.

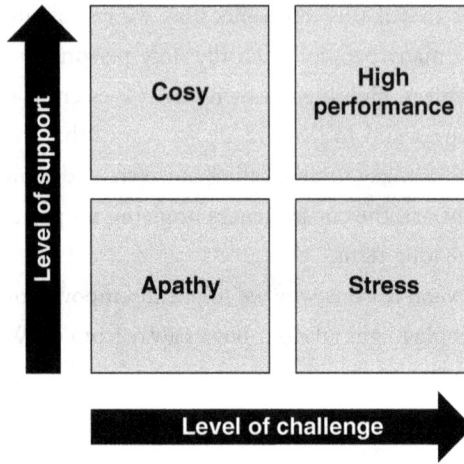

Figure 2.1 Sanford's support and challenge model

(Sanford, 1966)

In later chapters, we will see how we can develop an approach that is both supportive and challenging, that will help us achieve the things we really want to achieve.

Reason 2: It's Easier to Blame Others

Let's face it, if you let other people make decisions on your behalf, you have someone else to blame if it all goes wrong. If you made the decision yourself, and it doesn't work, you have nowhere else to look. The trouble with this approach is that it is still our responsibility if things didn't work out. After all, we made the decision to hand our power over to other people. So if it goes wrong, it remains our responsibility.

Reason 3: Lack of Self-Esteem or Confidence

It's sad but true. Many people have low self-esteem or lack self-confidence, often arising from loss of power at some point in the past. Because of this, we pass our power over to others voluntarily and allow them to run our lives. We allow more senior people to dictate our career direction. In addition, a lack of self-confidence makes us more vulnerable to other people taking our power away from us, whether we consented to it or not. The underlying belief here is that we are simply not good enough to run our own lives. So we choose to let other people run it instead.

Reason 4: We Assume Others Know More

This is the *expert* syndrome in action. In this case, we assume that other people are more expert than we are. For example, we may see doctors, solicitors, accountants, financial advisers, and others as the experts and defer to their judgment in making critical decisions on our behalf. However, this can also happen when people we know well adopt expert roles, for example:

- My partner is the one who is good with numbers.
- My work colleague has been in this job for longer than I have.
- My friend is a better judge of character than I am.

In the above examples, these people may genuinely be experts, or they may assume they are, or we may assign them the role of expert. However, the result is that we hand our power over to them to make decisions.

Reason 5: The "It's No Use Trying" Syndrome

In this case, we may have attempted to hold our power with particular people or situations but lost out. As a result, we give up on these areas of our life. Alternatively, we may have made some decisions in the past that didn't work out, so we assume we are incompetent in this area, and we pass our power over to someone else. We assume they are more competent than we are and that they will make decisions that are in our interest. Of course, it may not work out the way we hoped. For instance, we may have made a bad property decision in the past, and consequently we let someone else make these decisions for us in the future.

Reason 6: Fear

Good, old-fashioned fear can lead us to give up our power or to lose it forcibly to someone else. Some examples of fear would include:

- Fear of rejection—If I make a decision that other people don't approve of, they may choose to reject me and not like me. Fear of rejection from others is a powerful motivator that can stop us from taking decisions that are in our interest. Instead, we go for decisions that we think others will approve of and see as the *right* decision.
- Fear of failure—We may fear failure, if we take a risk, for example. Perhaps we were burned in the past, so we avoid taking chances. One of the biggest reasons why people don't go for what they really want is the fear of failure. It's better to set a lower target and then hit it than to set our sights high and risk missing.
- Fear of intimacy—Where we fear that baring our soul will lead to our being hurt, we will choose to keep it hidden from others. Thus, we disempower our emotional life. Where intimacy is a fear, we can find it almost impossible to develop a meaningful relationship with anyone.

Reason 7: Family Patterns

With family, power relationships will often persist long after the dependence is gone. For example, we may no longer depend on our parents for our survival, and in fact we might not even see them all that often. Yet we can go on for a long time depending on them for other things, like approval for what we're doing, or for our choice of partners. It's amazing how many successful business people I know who are great at handling all sorts of tricky situations—until their parents come along! Then they get caught in the subservient position, and the old patterns of behavior get played out. Old patterns are hard to change, making our families a key source of how we view and deal with power.

The irony of family and friends is that they can be our biggest allies in changing our lives for the better. But they can also be the very thing that holds us back, because they are used to us being where we are. If we try to change, that might be a threat to them.

Why Power Is Abused: The Surface Reasons

We have looked at some ways we may choose to disempower ourselves. However, the other side of the coin is that others may disempower you without your consent. Having done this, they are in a position of power over you.

Once this is the case, there are many reasons why people might resist giving up their power over you. These are generally to do with there being no compelling reason for them to change their behavior. Later in this book, we will look at how you can create a compelling reason for them to change this.

Here are just a few reasons why others won't change by themselves and hence why you might need to take charge of your own power yourself rather than rely on others to stop taking yours away.

Reason 1: It Gives Them Energy

Life is, in many ways, about acquiring energy to do things; many people see life as essentially a battle for energy. Imagine for a moment that you are a young child and have two brothers and a sister. Your parents must spread their energy around between the four of you. The more attention they get, the less is available for you, unless you push your case. You learn to fight for attention and to get your way.

If other people are taking your power to give themselves an energy boost, they are hardly likely to want to give it back to you. Of course, they might not realize the effect they are having on you, or they might not care. Either way, it leaves you with an issue to resolve.

Reason 2: There's a Sucker Born Every Day

People might justify holding power using this argument. If I think you are a sucker, then I can justify taking your power, as I will use it better than you. I think I am superior; therefore, I should be in charge. If people are stupid enough to let me take their power, then I will take it. Of course, this is a cynical view, and many people would never admit to holding a view like this. But that doesn't mean they don't hold a view like this in secret, and it will determine how they see your power, and their entitlement to it.

Reason 3: Sociopathic Tendencies

Sociopaths are individuals who exhibit antisocial personality disorder (ASPD). One definition of ASPD is as follows:

> . . . a pervasive pattern of disregard for, and violation of, the rights of others that begins in childhood or early adolescence and continues into adulthood.[2]

Deceit and manipulation are considered essential features of the disorder. According to the Personality Disorders Awareness Network, the diagnostic criteria for ASPD would include at least three of the following:

1. Repeated criminal acts
2. Deceitfulness
3. Impulsiveness
4. Repeated fights or assaults
5. Disregard for the safety of others
6. Irresponsibility
7. Lack of remorse[3]

Without going too far into defining sociopathic behavior, someone of this type is unlikely to respect your rights as an individual or treat you ethically. They may well be very aggressive in pursuing their goals. All of this, if you let them, will lead to your losing your power.

Sociopathic types can be remarkably successful in the workplace, as they are well equipped to operate in a ruthless, quick, political environment. These are qualities that are often encouraged at work.

Reason 4: The Need to Control

Some people have a high need to control events. Losing control over a situation is a source of great stress to them. Of course, in controlling events, this can lead directly to their attempting to control you as well. One classic case of this at work is the manager who wants to control everything going on in his or her department. You can guarantee that no one in his or her team will feel empowered. Indeed, they will feel quite the opposite.

Reason 5: It's for the Greater Good

Those holding power will often rationalize doing this as being necessary for the greater good. If I'm in this position, I might convince myself that I'm exercising power on behalf of everyone, so I can make decisions that are for the long-term good. This could be well-intentioned, of course. The only problem with this is that I might not know what your interests really are. Given this, how do I know your interests have been considered? I don't know, of course! What's worse, I might manipulate power to achieve my own ends while pretending I'm in favor of the common good. Even the biggest tyrants on the planet, like the recently deposed Robert Mugabe in Zimbabwe, often try to justify unfair, unethical, and murderous policies based on some notion of the common good.

Reason 6: Lack of Self-Awareness

In some cases, people might abuse my power simply because they aren't aware they are even doing it. They may simply be ignorant of what they are doing and its impact. They might be horrified if they were to be made aware of it. In these cases, simply pointing it out will help deal with the abuse of your personal power.

Reason 7: The Assumption That Silence Equals Consent

How many times have you been to a work meeting, when the manager announces some unpopular change? She asks if anyone has any questions about the announcement. Usually, no one asks anything. In fact, no one says anything at all. In the manager's eyes, this means that it's OK to go ahead. Silence can often be read as consent, especially when we don't really want to know how everyone else sees things, let alone how they feel about them.

℘

So, we have this paradox. Powerless people pounding the work, life, and family treadmills when they do have power to make some choices. We have never had as much opportunity to shape our own lives, and yet we behave as if we have no choice. What a waste of our own power, just given away. It is not without irony that Brene Brown was able to say the following:

> I think we're in a [time of a] lot of fear and scarcity. And I know that that's not new. What's new is that there are groups who are willing to leverage our fear—leveraging fear to get people to do what they want. We've lost our moral courage.[4]

Perhaps it's time that we took our moral courage back.

What Do I Mean by Ethical Power?

In this book, I am proposing that we use a strategy based on building our own ethical power base, to perform well in the workplace, and to live a great life. Let's define these terms a bit more elaborately.

Beginning with *power*, Dacher Keltner's definition, taken from the field of psychology, is as follows:

> In psychological science, power is defined as one's capacity to alter another person's condition or state of mind by providing or withholding resources—such as food, money, knowledge, and affection—or administering punishments, such as physical harm, job termination, or social ostracism.[5]

In other words, it is our ability to influence another person's decisions and actions through a combination of rewards and sanctions. This is the basis on which whole organizations and global companies operate. Without power, there would simply be chaos. As we will go on to see in the next chapter, there is more than one type of power.

As for the ethical component, why do ethics matter here? The word *ethical* has many different definitions that reflect many different professional, academic, social, cultural, and religious viewpoints. It is often easier to define *ethical* in its absence—we are far more able to identify unethical behavior. However, as a starting point, Business Dictionary defines ethical behavior as follows:

> Acting in ways consistent with what society and individuals typically think are good values. Ethical behavior tends to be good for business and involves demonstrating respect for key moral principles that include honesty, fairness, equality, dignity, diversity and individual rights.[6]

Keltner sums up succinctly his views on power when he states that "power is wielded most effectively when it's used responsibly by people who are attuned to, and engaged with, the needs and interests of others."[7]

This is a good summary of what *ethical power* is all about.

The Journey to Ethical Power

Holding power in our lives is a crucial factor if we are to achieve our potential. Without adequate use of our own ethical power, there can be no meaningful improvement in our capabilities and performance.

The journey to ethical power comprises nine key steps, from the simple recognition of power being an essential fact of life through to honestly recognizing our own lack of empowerment in different situations. These steps involve developing our own sense of direction, being willing and able to assert our power with other people, and then, finally, using our power ethically in the workplace and beyond.

A point that needs emphasis here is that the key steps are sequential for a reason: I don't believe it's possible to master a later step to ethical power unless the earlier ones have been mastered. It is generalizing a little to say that the earlier steps are to do with power, and the latter ones are to do with ethics. But this is generally the case. Earlier on, I voiced the concern that many people have about power; that power and ethics don't go together, and powerful people tend therefore to lack ethics.

I'd turn this view on its head. I believe it's impossible to be ethical without power. So, mastering the power bit is essential if we are to develop our ethical stance in any meaningful way. Spiritual people may not like this fact, but the world is not a monastery. It is a world of many different people doing many different things, and sometimes getting in each other's way. That makes self-empowerment an essential prerequisite for making a difference.

Given this point, each of the next nine chapters will develop another step on the road to ethical power. Each chapter will cover a discussion on what the step is about, along with some examples to highlight key principles. You will have the opportunity to apply each step through self-assessment and self-reflective exercises before moving onto the next step.

With this in mind, let's move to the first step to ethical power and begin the journey.

CHAPTER 3

The Inevitability of Power

Your time is limited—don't waste it living someone else's life.
—Steve Jobs

The first step to ethical power—Accept that power is inevitable

The first step to ethical power is to recognize power as an inevitable fact of life. Ignoring power doesn't make it go away. It just means you lose influence over your own life, putting it in the hands of others. Recognizing the different types of power can also be helpful.

Introduction: Power and Energy

Power is really inevitable in the workplace and in life. To be effective, we must exercise our own power. This is obvious when we look at the animal kingdom.

Think of a kitten, born into a litter of five. When it comes to feeding time, that kitten needs to find a way to its mother for milk. It is in competition for milk with the other four kittens. Nature will usually provide enough milk for all five kittens to live and grow. However, if some kittens are greedy, there may not be enough to go around. So our kitten may need to push its way in to get the milk it needs. If it doesn't, then it could eventually die. It certainly won't be as healthy as it could have been or grow up to be as strong. The runt of a litter does not survive in the wild.

For that kitten, getting to its mother is essential to acquiring energy for life. The link between power and energy is a crucial one. The kitten needs to use its power to get to the milk and gain more energy. And the kitten needs to use its energy to show enough power to get to the milk. Without energy, there is no power, and without power we don't acquire enough energy. This power–energy combination can be a virtuous or a vicious cycle.

Finding meaning in our career and in life requires us to influence what's going on around us, which means taking our own power and acknowledging the link between power and energy. The first step to ethical power is simply recognizing and coming to terms with this fact. Ignoring it does not move us forward, and as we will see in later chapters, the trick is to pursue ethical power and not to ditch power completely. Power is simply the application of energy to generate momentum. If we want to perform in our career and in our life, we must use our power.

Scarcity and Abundance

But then we don't live in the wild, do we? Oh, and most of us don't see ourselves as animals either. The trouble is, while we may be civilized (at least to an extent), scientists will confirm that our root behaviors remain essentially animalistic. What's more, our animal behavior will kick in more strongly when we perceive we are in competition for scarce resources that we see as essential to living.

Look at the scenario that takes place when two children fight over who gets a bar of chocolate or the bigger bit of the bar. There may be plenty of chocolates to go around. However, the principle of scarcity kicks in when both children may perceive (incorrectly) that there isn't enough. Adults are no better; just consider the driver who gets uptight with another driver who just sneaked into the only spare car parking space at the local supermarket. After all, it might take a whole 5 minutes before the driver sees another spare space become available. Disaster! Where we see scarcity rather than abundance, power becomes an inevitable issue.

That makes power and energy inevitable to living the moment we are born. Whenever we want something that has implications for other people, we are in a power situation. The principle of scarcity or perceived scarcity will result in power struggles. Now, I'm not suggesting that we pander to these animal instincts. Indeed, the test of civilized behavior is the degree to which we can move away from this base approach.

Sometimes there is genuine scarcity, as in a desert. But often in civilization we invent our own definition of scarcity when there is plenty to go around. This is worth bearing in mind when we choose to exert our power; is this *really* a situation of scarcity?

Of course, in work organizations, the scarcity challenge remains the same. Only one person can be promoted after all, and if one of my colleagues receives a budget for training, there might be less available for people like me!

Why We Avoid Power

Why do many people shy away from power? One key reason why many avoid it is that they simply see power as bad. This is the equation they have in their heads: *power equals bad*. You might have this equation in your mind, and it would be easy to see why you might think that way. For most people, bad is simply another word for unethical.

Consider the stories we hear in the media, stories of Church abuse of children and Hollywood abuse of women, stories of our elected representatives milking the public purse for their own benefit, stories of banking bonuses and dodgy behavior in the stock markets around the world, and so on. All cases of power being abused by those in power.

It is no different in the workplace. We hear stories of workplace bullying and its consequences, whistle-blowers being fired for daring to speak up, pension funds for employees being raided, employees being unfairly (and illegally) dismissed, environmentally catastrophic business behavior, and bribes being given and taken. You get the picture.

One quote I love sums up many people's view of power. Jon Wynne-Tyson, a British author and publisher, commented that "the wrong sort of people are always in power because they would not be in power if they were not the wrong sort of people."[1]

I smiled when I read this for the first time because it summed up perfectly my own view of power at that time. It comes as no surprise then that in those days, I avoided power in my life as many people do. Indeed, for more years than I care to remember, I actively avoided positions of power and said more than once that "I prefer influence to power."

The trouble with taking this view is that failing to use our own power will mean that we won't be effective, either professionally or personally. We will go to the grave wondering if things could have been different.

The key to Step 1 to ethical power is to adopt a more positive view of power than the one we are encouraged by the media and those in power to adopt. We should remember the likes of Martin Luther King, Nelson Mandela, and Mohandas Gandhi. No one can deny how powerful they were, and few would deny that they were immensely ethical with it. They empowered themselves and in turn were able to empower others.

Power is essential to achieving great things in the workplace. The only question is whether we choose to see that or not.

Your experience as a young child will be an important determinant of your attitude to power. After all, as a young child, we are virtually powerless. We are surrounded by authoritative figures: parents, relatives, and other adults. They literally have the power of life and death over us. Many of the ways we deal with people in power are formed early in our lives. You may have already realized some of these patterns, but not all of them.

Given the above, getting a clearer perspective on your attitude to power is important. That is what we will do next.

Exercise: My Attitude to Power

This is an opportunity to consider your own attitudes and approaches to power. You will need to write on something for this, to work through the following questions.

1. Make a list of words that describe your attitude to power and to people (including yourself) using power.
2. Out of the words you've just written, how many of them are positive words? How many of them are negative? Take note of the balance of positive and negative words you've used. Which category is the biggest one?

3. From your childhood, describe the first experience you had with power that you remember.
4. What did that experience teach you? How did this color your attitude and approach to power later in life?

ഇ

As a child, you would have experienced being on the receiving end of different types of power, which would have influenced you to varying degrees. Adults will have power because of their position, in their role as your parents. They also controlled resources such as food and pocket money. You may have seen your parents as experts or as wise, and you may have liked and loved them.

As adults, we experience power in different ways. Let's have a look at the different types of power in our lives, particularly in the workplace.

Types of Power

There are five main types of power we face and can have in business life, and indeed more generally. These are based on work carried out by psychologists John French and Bertram Raven.[2] The five types are reward, coercive, legitimate, referent, and expert. Let's consider each of them in more detail, bearing in mind that we may have more than one type of power in play at any one time; in other words, the sources of power do overlap in modern organizational life.

Reward Power

This is the power to reward people for doing what we want. It is tied in to resources we control that others may want access to, for example money, materials, or people. In the workplace, managers may hold considerable reward power, from awarding a pay rise and bonus to giving out desirable projects as a reward, to praising the work of staff. I have reward power when I have control of a resource that could be helpful to you, and I let you have access to it if you do what I want. Resources could include money, ownership, or command of key people. Outside work, parents have reward power to treat their children or hand over pocket money, while bank managers can choose to let you have a loan or refuse it.

Coercive Power

This is our capacity to penalize or sanction people for noncompliance with our wishes. We use the fear of a penalty or loss to compel compliance from people. Some managers in smaller organizations (and a few larger ones!) may use the threat of dismissal to get compliance from their staff.

Among his many overlapping sources of power, Steve Jobs famously used his coercive power to shout and threaten to get rid of employees at Apple that he saw as underperforming in some way. I will return to Steve Jobs again shortly.

Legitimate Power

This is the power we hold by virtue of our job title at work or sometimes elsewhere, for example in our family (e.g., head of family) or in other organizations we are involved with. This is where power overlaps with authority. When we have legitimate power, we have the authority to make legitimate requests of other people. For example, as a line manager, I can use my authority to ask my staff to do things that are part of their job description and employment contract. The organization I work for has given me authority (i.e., permission) to do this.

In a similar vein, a teacher, minister, or bank manager can hold considerable legitimate power.

While this is an important source of power, it is often not sufficient on its own. For instance, in the mid-1990s in Britain, John Major's Conservative government was in power but was struggling for its survival. One minister in the government famously described Major's position as being "in office, but not in power."[3] Major had the legitimate power, but little else at the time. He subsequently lost all power at the 1997 general election.

Referent Power

This is the personal power that comes from us as individual human beings. It can sometimes be referred to as charisma or gravitas. This source of power derives from our person or personality. People who are charismatic, engaging, great communicators, visionary, and good listeners will carry great personal power. One of the best examples of personal power was Mohandas Gandhi who provided the inspiration for Indian independence in 1947. He engaged with people, connected with their hopes and fears, and was one of the greatest leaders of the 20th century. Yet he was never the Indian Prime Minister—Nehru held that job, but not as many people remember him. The reason for this is that Gandhi held great referent power to influence people's hearts and minds. Nehru, for all his qualities, held other sources of power (e.g., legitimate and reward) but had less referent power.

We will notice this in our own lives too. People who are great at winning us over to their viewpoint, talking us round, and great charmers can be great manipulators too if we're not careful.

Expert Power

We may have power because we are or are perceived as an expert in an area. We gain this by building up our knowledge and skill. Many traditional trades in manufacturing and elsewhere relied on expertise as the main source of power. For example, knowing the right temperature to heat molten steel to achieve maximum strength. Accountants, IT professionals, human resources, and legal professionals all rely on expertise as a key source of power in organizations.

Power can derive from expertise when you are seen or assumed by others to have particular expertise. In this case, your advice is likely to carry some weight in what people do. We encounter experts in all walks of life too—teachers, bank managers, solicitors, financial advisers, family planning experts, IT experts, car mechanics, and so on.

One thing that experts often do to consolidate their power is to rely on intellectualization or *big words* to baffle others. This can make them appear even more *expert* and increase both our reliance on them and their power over us. Obscure terms and jargon are the common currency of experts.[4]

Combining the Sources of Power

I have already mentioned Steve Jobs for famously utilizing the coercive power source in bawling out his staff when things went wrong or when he thought they weren't doing their jobs properly. However, he also demonstrates how to get the most out of each source of power and then combine them to achieve great results.

He had ample reward power, from his ability as CEO of Apple to recruit talent and reward it through salary, bonuses, praise, and the opportunity to be involved in cutting-edge IT projects. He held great legitimate power from being CEO to determine the direction of both business and employees. He held great referent power from his ability to be charismatic and hold audiences spellbound, from Apple product launches to addressing graduates about life lessons. Finally, who can dispute his expert power, given the impact his inventions and innovations had on the world of work and play?

In short, Steve Jobs maxed out on all five sources of power, and the result quite literally is he changed the world. How many people can truly claim that?

Exercise: What Power Do I Use?

What types of power do you utilize in your daily activities? Where do your preferred sources of power come from?

Think about your working activities. For each of these sources of power, write down the extent to which you could use it to enable you to perform effectively. Then write down the extent to which you either use this source of power or avoid it? In other words, I'm asking you to conduct a power audit on yourself.

Which sources of power do you tend to defer to when you need to use power? Reward, coercive, legitimate, referent, or expert? We all have our favorites, but which are yours?

Finally, which ones do you either avoid using at all or use only as a last resort?

∽

The key to exercising power effectively is to maximize our use of these different types of power. Being aware of where our potential power lies is important. In terms of self-empowerment, the key source of power is the referent one. Truly powerful people maximize in this category. There is some evidence that the stronger the professional focus an individual has, the more significant an influence referent power has compared to the other sources.

You also need to become more aware of how others are exercising their power, particularly when it has an impact on your own.

Summary

In this chapter, we have explored the first principle of ethical power, which is to recognize that power is essential to our own personal effectiveness. You have explored some of your attitudes and approaches to power and looked at five different sources of power. You have also identified the types of power you use and avoid using. You have probably realized that you are comfortable with some sources of power more than others.

Looking at your own approach to power in the past can be helpful. However, it's equally important that we can assess our own power at the present time. The second step to ethical power will deal with how we do this.

CHAPTER 4

Noticing Your Power

When I want your opinion, I'll give it to you.

—Laurence J. Peter

The second step to ethical power—Notice how you feel in the moment

The second step to ethical power is to connect to your feelings in the moment as key to working out whether your power is being exercised or undermined. There are several telltale signs that you are losing your own power. Noticing them will tell you your current state of power, and this is crucial as power is often used and misused subtly.

Introduction: Notice How You Feel

How do you feel about the way your career is going? What about your life? Are you happy and performing well? Are you fed up and disappointed? Are you somewhere in between? How do you feel about particular events you have faced? Just consider this example from the workplace, building on the first scenario from Chapter 1:

My name is Gary, and I'm walking in for a project team meeting. A scene like this is enacted every week, and it is one that I absolutely dread. It is a 2-hour business meeting with work colleagues and my manager, who loves the sound of his own voice. The aim of the project is to improve the full customer experience, from beginning to end. The customer first initiative will form part of this, and my responsibility is to make sure we do this in a way that complies with financial services

(Continued)

regulation. As I mentioned, Tony, my manager, is chairing the project team. Therefore, it is no surprise that I end up doing most of the work.

No doubt today I'll be asked to account for what I'd done since last week's meeting. If previous experience is anything to go by, it will feel like a trial, and I will be corrected in public for everything that isn't completed to everyone else's satisfaction.

I won't go through the full tedium of this meeting, but the following is a good cameo of what happens. My boss asked me how my action point was going in documenting existing procedure when a customer switches investment funds for their personal pension. I replied that it was in hand, I just needed to have a meeting with Alan, who is also on the project team. I need his help to do this as he oversees fund switches in pensions; he knows more detail than I do on the subject. In fact, come to think of it, Alan should be doing the work, with me helping him.

Tony steamed in with "why has it taken this long for you to talk to Alan?" He then looks at both of us. Alan chimes in with it's no problem, "let's sit down and sort it out tomorrow morning. 10 o'clock OK?" I mumbled "yes, that's fine." The meeting moved on to the next agenda point, but why is it I feel like I'm not doing my job? Why couldn't Alan be this helpful when I mentioned having a meeting a few days ago? Oh, he was too busy then to bother with me.

You can apply the second step to ethical power at any time. The key to it is simply to start noticing how you feel in the present moment. Notice how you feel, whatever you are doing—preparing for a meeting, talking to someone, traveling, or whatever. Taking note of your feelings at that point in time will give you lots of data to assess your own state of power.

The basic equation is simple:

- Where we feel good, we are likely to be empowered and energized.
- Where we feel bad, we are disempowered. We may feel drained or low energy at these times.

The biggest single step you can take to enhance your own power is to become aware of your moods and emotions in the moment or at least as close to the moment as possible. Your current mood or emotion tells you something about your own state of mind, which is closely associated with your state of power. Once you are aware of this and feel a power loss going on, you can then decide what to do about it.

Scenario: Project Meeting

The following coaching interview provides an example of the second step to ethical power in action. The individual in question is Gary, who we've just heard from in the above example. He is discussing the forthcoming project team meeting that he's about to have with Tony and the rest of the team:

"What was going through your head as you got ready for that meeting?"

"My thoughts before they arrived? Well, I wasn't looking forward to it. I expected the usual questions and comments about aspects of my performance, probably a few sarcastic comments about the project. To be honest, I was dreading the meeting. I felt anxious and uptight."

"And how did you feel, Gary, as the meeting wore on?"

"Fed up, annoyed at being put on the spot, just wishing it was over. I lost the will to live."

"Not good feelings then?"

"No."

"And how would you describe your level of power on this occasion?"

"Pathetic, low, out of power. It felt like everyone else was in control, and I was not."

"So, summarizing what you've said, you felt bad, and you had no power."

"Yes, that summarizes it all pretty well."

There lies the case for noticing the link between our emotions and our power. If you feel bad, that's a good sign if you choose to notice it. Your feelings are telling you that you're losing your power. Once you realize this, you can do something about it.

Exercise: Recent Key Events

It can be useful to go through the same review exercise that Gary did in the above example. So, get something to write on and work through the following questions for yourself.

1. Think about an event or incident where you felt bad at the time. Who were you with, and what was going on? Put your mind back to the time this happened. It doesn't matter whether the event was big or small.
2. Now try to pin exactly what the feeling was. Annoyance? Irritation? Drained? Angry? Write down the feeling you experienced.
3. In hindsight, in what way do you think you were losing your power? Who—or what—were you losing it to?
4. Now cast your mind back to a recent event or incident where you felt good at the time. Who were you with, and what was happening? Put your mind fully back into how it felt being in that event.
5. What was the feeling you experienced? Happiness? Optimistic? Confident? Full of energy? Describe what it was.
6. In what way, do you think you were gaining power or being empowered? How was that happening?

The 10 Signs of Power Loss

The thing about power is that it isn't always easy to see where we have lost it at the time. Often, we lose our power in subtle ways, making it less obvious when we're losing it or have lost it.

In these enlightened times, it is generally viewed as unacceptable to blatantly undermine another person's power. However, the one thing about naked exercise of power is that at least you are painfully aware that your rights are being violated. That makes it easier to then decide what, if anything, you do about it. When the approach is subtler, it might be less obvious to us that our rights and power are being taken away from us. So, we risk allowing our power to be removed by stealth.

There are many feelings that would tell us when we're losing power or have lost it completely—for example, dread, irritability, annoyance, or losing the will to keep going. Here are 10 signs that might indicate when we are losing our power.

Sign 1: Lethargy and Tiredness

It's always possible that we could be genuinely lethargic or low energy on a particular day. We could be suffering from a virus, infection, or just be tired. However, if this is happening to us consistently, then it is a sign of power loss. In addition, if we can work out when it is that we are losing our energy and feeling tired, we should be able to work out what is draining our power. So, for example, is it:

- We feel tired first thing on a Monday morning.
- We feel lethargic when faced with a visit to someone in particular.

Have you ever noticed how people are full of energy when they have something to go for but lose it when others deflate their enthusiasm?

Power and energy are brothers in arms. So, if our energy level is consistently low, then that suggests something or someone is draining and disempowering us.

Sign 2: That Sinking Feeling

You're in a situation, and you notice that sinking feeling. This means you should consider in what way your power is being undermined. It may mean that things are not going your way, and your power is coming into conflict with another person or people. It may be a situation that brings your feeling out (e.g., finding yourself in a conflict). It could be a specific person who has this impact on you (e.g., your manager).

Noticing this feeling when it occurs is important if you are to consider how it is you may be giving up your own power. The feeling may often be accompanied by the sense that we are in some way *small* compared to the other person and that our power is literally draining away.

Sign 3: Dread

Dread has many similarities to the sinking feeling and one main difference. The difference is that a sinking feeling takes place during the situation in question, whereas dread occurs in anticipation of it. So, we may dread going to see our boss at work because last time we did so, we had a bad time. The last thing we want is another bad time, so we end up dreading the next visit.

The irony about dread is that often we end up getting what we expect. A sense of dread means we are likely to prepare less well and less confidently for a situation. That makes us less likely to achieve what we want and probably more likely to get what we don't want.

Many people experience this feeling in the run up to visits from relations, for example at Christmas. How much of this feeling is down to you losing your personal power in situations like this?

Sign 4: Focusing on the Trivial

How much time do you spend looking at the trivial things, that don't add much to your personal effectiveness or quality of life? "I must get the filing done now" or "That's not the right kind of paperclip!"

One thing is for sure. If we use our power on trivial stuff, then by implication we're not using it on the big things. If we look at what people nearing the end of their life would say by way of advice, they would advise not to spend our time on trivialities and concentrate on the big things. Yet it's amazing how many people ignore this advice. Take one look at any letters page in a magazine, at the complaints raised in the workplace, or at tweets read out on TV programs, and you will find loads of examples of people wasting their time on trivialities.

Many people get caught up in following celebrities. Perhaps one reason for the rise of reality TV has been down to people needing to escape their reality, which is disempowered. After all, if I can vote for the winner of *Big Brother* or *Pop Idol*, then I must have some power.

You do, but what are you achieving by using this power? It's no better than a prisoner being in charge of his prison cell. If you spend your time worrying about the color of your cell walls, then take a good, hard look at what you're doing.

Sign 5: Extreme Interests

How many people do you know who have an extreme interest in sport? They are fanatical about their team and will sulk for days if they lose a game? How many people do you know who spend every Saturday in retail therapy? They spend a fortune on more clothes than they could possibly wear. Even if they need nothing, they are still found in the shopping malls around the world.

How many people do you know who watch every film starred in by a specific actor or actress or know everything that ever happened in a *Star Wars* film and go to all the conventions?

An extreme interest in this way may signify attention being diverted from stuff that really matters in our work and lives. If we are empowered at work and more generally, then while we may still have other interests, they are less likely to be this obsessive.

Sign 6: That Treadmill Feeling

Does your job resemble a treadmill? Do you feel as though you are running around day after day, just trying to keep up, not getting anywhere? Your day, week, month, and even year consists of loads of activities, and at the end of that time you are basically back where you started. You have no time to devote to things that would raise your game or to projects that you really do want to spend time on. If you feel like this, then you are losing your power and probably working to other people's agendas. Some disempowered people cover it up by engaging in lots of activity. This approach confuses activity with power; after all, if I am busy, then I matter. However, it may be activity rather akin to a mouse frantically running around a wheel. How many people do you see at work who always appear to be busy? But are they being a busy fool?

This feeling of being on the treadmill is different from busy people who feel that they are making progress in their lives. After all, a treadmill can be a good thing, but only if it is going in the right direction. If it's going in the wrong direction, then your power is being lost somewhere. Running fast just to stand still is a sure sign of this.

Sign 7: Gossip and Humor

Gossip and humor can be fun and is a good way to let off tension. But it can also be a telltale sign that power is absent. Take, for example, the sarcastic comment about work or the satirical joke about the boss. When this humor is present, it usually means the following factors are in play:

1. There are people who disagree with the direction being taken.
2. They are, or feel, powerless to do anything about it or even to say anything about it.
3. They wish to let off steam, and somehow let their view be known.

Humor can be used to minimize the impact of a situation ("oh I'll get over it") or to defuse a situation that feels unpleasant by laughing it off rather than confront the issue at hand. Even more damaging is when the humor is at our own expense, like "ah well, that shows how bad my memory is!"

Overall then, humor is often a sign that power is being sacrificed.

Sign 8: Frustration and Temper Loss

We can become frustrated at our lack of progress, poor results, or with our whole life. It can arise from a sense that we are not getting anywhere. Frustration is more of a low burn, chronic summary of how we feel about our circumstances. However, a more acute version of frustration can arise in response to specific triggers; at this point, we lose our temper. We can lose it over relatively minor things, for example, missing a bus or our computer taking too long to boot up. We snap at the people nearby; they didn't necessarily cause our frustration, but they are a convenient target for our frustration or temper. Many people vent when they arrive home from work, having experienced a buildup of frustration during the day.

So, if you continually feel frustrated about something, or you lose your temper regularly, stop to think about what is causing this. It may well be an area of your life where you have lost your power.

Sign 9: Alcohol, Eating, Our Body, and Physical Appearance

The signs of unhappy people are all around us. People who drink too much alcohol. People who put on weight and eat the wrong things. People who don't bother to exercise and become unfit. People who don't take trouble on their own appearance. If you fit any of these categories, what is this saying about you, and what's missing from your life? These are signs that people have given up on something, heading instead to consolation activities. And if it feels like you have little to look forward to, then what's the point in looking good?

Have you ever come across someone who had a healthy diet, drank moderately, exercised, and looked after themselves? Then one day they stopped doing so? This is a sign of something being wrong with their work, life, or relationships. What was it that was taken away from them? What caused it? Whatever the cause is, power loss won't be far away. If you don't believe this, look at the TV programs on diet and drink, when overweight people are interviewed. Apart from bad dietary habits, one common factor they tend to share is low self-esteem. So, either they gave their self-esteem away or somebody else took it.

Sign 10: We Don't Feel Ourselves

Here, we may feel out of sorts, unwell, or not ourselves. Illness is just one example of the body saying *something is wrong*. There is plenty of evidence for the idea that if the mind remains unhealthy for long enough, the body will eventually follow.

Alternatively, instead of being unwell, we may feel out of sorts, almost as if we aren't entirely in our own head. In this case, we end up observing our lives almost as a detached party. If we aren't in our head, we aren't taking full responsibility for ourselves. So, who is?

Part of not feeling ourselves could be a sense that we are not living our life in line with what's important to us. We will come back to this point later in the book.

Exercise: My Default Signs of Power Loss

Which of these 10 signs do you show when you lose your own power? To complete this exercise, you will need something to write on.

1. Review each of the above 10 signs that indicate loss of power. We all have our favorites, which ones are yours? List the signs that you've displayed over the years.
2. Write down one example from your past where you showed one or more of the above signs as a result of losing your power. What was it that caused your reaction?
3. What conclusions do you draw from what you have written?

လ

There we have it, the 10 signs that we have lost, or are losing, our power to influence our own priorities. These signs become even more important if we have become desensitized about our own feelings. All of which leads me on to a key point about this, which is a variation of the British stiff upper lip, and near wartime mantra of *Stay Calm and Keep Going*. I'm talking about the words *OK* and *fine*.

Avoidance of Feelings

How many times do you get, in response to the question *how are you today?* the reply *OK* or *fine* or even *alright?* You may even use these words yourself. I've known more people than I can remember, facing events like relationship collapse, redundancy, even bereavement, who when you ask them how they are or how they feel, answer with one of these words. In what way could they possibly be feeling OK, alright or fine? I doubt if they were, but these words are a signal that the individual may be desensitized to their own feelings. I've even used them myself in the past.

These words mean nothing. Nothing at all. It's just another way of in effect, saying to the other person "I don't want to talk about this, let's talk about something else." If this describes you, then it's time to develop a wider vocabulary to describe how you are and how you're feeling. Otherwise, you are anaesthetizing yourself against acknowledging how you really feel, which means you are losing a key barometer to your state of power at any time. It means you are traveling on the journey through life without a compass.

Case Study: The Flatline Manager

Not being attuned to our own feelings undermines our credibility. A great example of this was the manufacturing manager who attended an authentic leadership course alongside managers from other businesses. During an exercise designed to talk about the high and low points of his career (and indeed his life), he described his emotional state of mind as 6 or 7 out of 10 for the entire duration of his career, which had spanned 20 years. In other words, for his entire life, he had basically been *OK* or *alright*!

Now, this is unlikely to have been the case, as he had been through business restructures, hadn't always been successful in getting jobs that he'd applied for, and had been bereaved in his personal life. However, it was the reaction from his fellow managers that was the most telling thing in this case study; they asked him how he was fit to lead other people if this was how he experienced life. How do you lead people through change if you are so emotionally stunted yourself? The lack of awareness this manager had of his own feelings completely undermined his credibility with his colleagues in one moment of time.

Exercise: My Power Awareness

The more attuned we are to our feelings, the better able we become to assess our state of power in the moment. As an exercise, consider the following list of feelings, and tick off all those you know you have felt over the last 5 years. How many are there?

The feelings are classified into three main categories for convenience. The good feelings would suggest either that you were empowered at the time or that you were fine with whatever was happening at the time. The second category is warning signals, which suggest that your state of power is under challenge, either from yourself (e.g., doing something to undermine yourself) or from other people or situations. The third category is bad feelings, which suggest a state of disempowerment (Table 4.1).

Table 4.1 List of feelings

Good	Warning signals	Bad
Agreeable	Anxious	Alienated
Alive	Bored	Annoyed
Bold	Challenged	Ashamed
Calm	Concerned	Bitter
Cheerful	Disappointed	Depressed
Confident	Dissatisfied	Diminished
Content	Empty	Discouraged
Courageous	Fatigued	Disillusioned
Curious	Fed up	Down
Delighted	Frustrated	Embarrassed
Determined	Impatient	Fearful
Dynamic	Indecisive	Guilty
Elated	Indignant	Helpless
Encouraged	Irritated	Hopeless
Energetic	Isolated	Hurt
Excited	Lost	Incapable
Free	Nervous	Inferior
Great	Preoccupied	Intimidated
Happy	Provoked	Miserable
Inspired	Reassured	Overwhelmed
Jubilant	Rebellious	Paralyzed
Liberated	Relieved	Pessimistic
Optimistic	Smart	Powerless
Playful	Suspicious	Resentful
Pleased	Tense	Sad
Proud	Uneasy	Scared
Respected	Vulnerable	Unhappy
Satisfied	Wary	Upset
Wonderful	Worried	Useless

Having ticked off the feelings that applied to you, now consider the following questions:

1. How many did you tick in each category? What does that suggest about your state of power?
2. Now pick two feelings, either from the *warning signal* or *bad* categories. What was it that happened to prompt your feelings?
3. What did you say to yourself about how you felt at the time?
4. What did you say to other people about how you felt, if anything?

The Subtlety of Modern Power

Cast your mind back one to two hundred years ago, and what society was like. For a start, most people had no vote. Universal suffrage was still a long way away. Then consider work. You might work in a factory or on a farm. If you weren't the personal property of the owner, then at the very least your boss literally had the power of life and death over you. Step out of line, and you'd lose your job—there was no employment protection in those days, and no welfare provision. Without your job, you'd lose your home. Life was black and white. Obey the owner or be cast out onto the street. But that's not all. Your family upbringing would have been strict. Step out of line, and you could expect to be beaten by your parents and relatives. If other grown-ups spoke to you, you listened to them and did what they told you. At school, you could expect the worst if you stepped out of line. Even failing school tests or exams could be reason enough to expect to be punished. And if your parents found out that you'd been in trouble at school, you could expect to be in trouble at home too.

The only acceptable relationship for bringing up a family was marriage, and within that marriage, the man was unequivocally in charge. It was even seen as acceptable for the man to beat his wife if she stepped out of line. Homosexuality and love outside wedlock were forbidden.

It was all clear cut, and in many ways that's the point. There is no way you could describe this life as fair; life was incredibly hard and very unfair. Real power was held by those in authority—capitalists, church leaders, teachers, and within the home the husband or father. Everyone else was relatively disempowered. But, in one respect, at least things were clear. You knew where you had power, and you knew where you didn't. There was no scope for debate, where power lay was obvious. Where you were not in power, you could still make a choice, to comply with authority or rebel against it. Rebellion often carried grave consequences, but you could choose to rebel. Whether you complied or rebelled, at least you had a clear choice to make, and you were clear about how much power you had.

It's not like that nowadays. We all have a vote, even if at times it doesn't seem to matter. We're raised in all sorts of families—two parent, single parent, step parents, even occasionally gay parents. Schools are more participative and democratic, with corporal punishment long ago outlawed. Even at home, child beatings are largely history, thankfully. Indeed, even in my lifetime, being banished to your room has gone from being a punishment to almost being a reward. When I was a child, all the entertainment was to be found in the living room—TV, computer, video. Nowadays, the son of one of my friends has more technology in his room than I had in my first flat!

Work is more democratic, at least on the surface. I've lost track of the number of empowerment initiatives I've seen, not to mention employee engagement surveys, all the emphasis on the opportunity to manage our own careers and work consultation initiatives. It can take forever for an employer to get rid of even a bad employee, unless they do something stupid like get caught stealing.

So, it's all a bit muddy nowadays, less clear cut, and less obvious when you have power and when you don't have power. At times, it's less obvious where the power lies. The thing about power in modern society is that it isn't always easy to see where we have lost it at the time. Often, other people are subtle in taking it away from us, making any transgression less obvious.

For example, let's say that at work, I have a new boss. It is unlikely nowadays that she will say to me *do it my way or take the highway!* Instead, she will more likely suggest her ways of doing things. She might say I can do it a different way if I want. But I know that, if I do, I will get it in the neck if it goes wrong. On the other hand, do it her way and I am more protected if it goes wrong. Which option will I take? The pressure may be subtle, but the pressure is on for me to do it her way.

Much of the language in modern society is of individual empowerment. However, it sometimes disguises the reality for many people of being quite disempowered.

For a more humorous example of modern disempowerment, consider the contact center. They are designed to enable calls to be dealt with more efficiently, or so we are told. Have you ever experienced a situation like this? Behind the laughter, many of us will have experienced something like this and what it does to our power.

Case Study: Being the Customer

What is it about call centers? Lucy and I were whiling away our Sunday around the house when Lucy discovers a problem with our broadband Internet connection. That means we also have a problem with our phone line and the cable TV service. After a brief conversation, we agree that I should phone the company to complain. So, that is what I do.

The steps I go through are as follows:

Step 1: I dial the phone number for the company. The number rings out several times, longer than I'd reasonably expect.

Step 2: The phone is eventually answered by an automated message. I encounter that brief pause, before a voice, which tells me in advance that this is indeed going to be an automated message.

Step 3: The voice tells me to press one if you want X, two if you want Y, three if you want Z, and to hold the line if it's anything else I need. None of these options is what I really want, so I hold on the line. Nothing further happens for a while.

Step 4: My call gets put through to another phone. This phone rings out for a while and is eventually answered by another automated message.

Step 5: This message tells me to press one for A, press two for B, press three for C, and press four for D. For any other questions, please hold. By this time, the coffee that Lucy made me is cold.

Step 6: I hold. I know by now that I am in a queue for a bucket of different questions that could be about anything. In other words, I am unlikely to have my phone call answered now by a readymade expert. The experts are all answering the phones linked to options one to four.

Step 7: My call is finally answered by a human being! I relay my complaint about the broadband connection being faulty. Unfortunately, the customer care adviser, Russell, requests two ID numbers I've never heard of and cannot find at this point. Consequently, I must hang up and find them.

(*Continued*)

Step 8: Having located the ID numbers in question, I repeat Steps 1–6 above in their entirety and ask Lucy if she would kindly make me another coffee.

Step 9: This time, my call is answered by Sardeep, who appears not to know the Russell I spoke to not 15 minutes ago. Presumably, Russell has by now left the company.

Step 10: I relay my complaint in its entirety again, and this time I add in the two ID numbers that I know will be required. I answer questions about Lucy's mother's maiden name, my first pet, our postcode, Lucy's date of birth, and the names of the last 10 Popes, along with length of reign. Meanwhile, my coffee appears from a clearly amused Lucy. She does not understand how stressed I am.

Step 11: Sardeep asks me if I have unplugged the phone line and replugged it in, as well as switching the control box off, letting it cool down, and switching it on again. I stupidly say no, leading him to suggest I do this first, as it usually cures the problems I'm having. He leaves me with little choice but to hang up again.

Step 12: I switch the box off and unplug the phone line for 10 minutes. Then I plug back in and switch on. I check the situation, and the broadband problem is still there. By this time, my smartphone battery is low, so I plug in the charger before I call back. Lucy asks for, and takes, my lunch order.

Step 13: I repeat Steps 1–6 in their entirety, and smile at Lucy, the sort of smile that says *I wish you were doing this, and I was making lunch.*

Step 14: This time, my call is answered by Elaine, who is clueless as to the saga that has been unfolding this last hour. I put her right and suggest some novel ways her company might like to store customer information in future. Elaine tells me she is sorry I feel like this, but that it's not her fault and she would like to help me if possible. I fume.

Step 15: I tell her the story of what's wrong yet again. I give her the two ID numbers before she thinks to ask for them. I answer several security questions yet again. Two of them are different—my mother's maiden name this time and my favorite sports team. But I am still awaiting the question on Werner Heisenberg's uncertainty principle. I'm baffled why it hasn't been asked, as uncertainty seems all the rage on this phone call.

Step 16: I tell her that I have switched everything off and unplugged everything when she asks me, and it still doesn't work. I'm ready for that question this time.

Step 17: Elaine tells me it sounds like I have a problem then. I fall off my chair, while Lucy simultaneously arrives with a plate of sandwiches.

Step 18: Elaine tells me she will arrange for an engineer to visit. I'm away from home these next 2 days. I need to check with Lucy whether and when she can be at home for a visit. Lucy cooperates fully, and I tell Elaine when she can be around.

Step 19: Elaine tells me that the engineering booking system is down just now, so she cannot commit at this point to a definite time. If we can call back later or tomorrow morning, she will be able to confirm a time. In the meantime, she will put us down for an engineer's visit.

Step 20: I ask what the odds are that she will answer the phone later when I call back or will it be Timmy, Hussein, or Samantha. I add that I now need a new mobile phone, as this one is worn out.

When I hang up, Lucy is in hysterics. Despite the huge inconvenience, I too see the funny side of it, but only once I calm down.

The above example is intended to be an amusing account. However, what it highlights to me is the way that business organizations systematically disempower normal people by making it difficult to get any contact with anyone who works for them. You used to be able to make one phone call to get someone, but not anymore. Contact centers even regulate the questions you are supposed to ask. I remember a recent example where it took me 6 months to cancel a contract with one organization because they made it almost impossible to do it. For one thing, there were no call center or online options if you wanted to cancel!

There's much to say about the lack of customer service or indeed about how difficult it is to talk to another human being. However, my main point centers on power. Many businesses make it very difficult nowadays for us to exercise our power. If our call isn't a standard one, we have no idea whom to ask to talk to. Staff who work in contact centers often have a target to get us off the line as quickly as possible, so they can deal with the next call. There are many ways that organizations can disempower us, and call centers are just one example.

Disempowerment in an Empowered Disguise

Much of the conversation around work–life balance implies that it's a matter of individual choice. We can choose our own personal balance to suit our lifestyle. Who really believes this?

The issue may be presented as a choice and lifestyle one. In practice, most people who talk to me about work–life balance are simply wishing they had more space for their life, as there is too much work. Evening work, weekend work, and having smartphones and work laptops means being on call for work, even when we're at home. This is on top of the epidemic of *zero-hour* contracts, where people are expected to be on call, even if they might not be needed.

Consider another sign of *progress* in the last 40 years, the emancipation of working mothers. Until the early 1960s, the norm in society was for dad to go to work and mum to stay at home and look after the children. As we all know, this has changed. Much of the propaganda emphasizes the benefits to women of being able to work, and at least officially, women have the same rights at work as men. All this is good and represents progress. But let's consider the issue from another angle.

How many families can afford to have only one wage earner? In 1960, most households ran in this way. Now, it's an economic necessity to have both partners working—a house can no longer run on only one salary. Two salaries are usually needed now to make a living and increasing numbers of people need more than one job to do so.

The economist Richard Wolff[1] estimated that, between 1979 and 2009, the average wage per hour for the average worker declined in real terms in the United States. This decline was masked until the economic recession at the end of this period by several factors, which included people taking second jobs, more women working, extended working hours, and borrowing on mortgages and credit.

What this means, of course, is that women must work to keep their households financially afloat; that's hardly the lifestyle choice we are told it is. Consider for yourself just how empowering a situation this is.

The language of empowerment is all around us, but it often disguises a reality of disempowerment. When blatant exercise of power is replaced by subtle exercise of power, it becomes less obvious to us that our rights and power are being removed. So, we risk allowing our power to be taken by stealth.

Therefore, it is important to be aware of our feelings, emotions, and moods. Our feelings are an invaluable indication of our state of power in the moment. They tell you when you're powerful, being manipulated, or put down upon, even if it's less obvious to your rational brain.

Optimism and Pessimism: The Law of Resonance

"Oh dear, definitely a pessimist. The glass for him is empty, broken, and there's no prospect of any other glass at any point in the future."

Have you ever come across this type? The sort who always focuses on the negatives, the limitations, and the drawbacks? The type whose sense of humor, if one exists, is either cynical or sarcastic—putting situations or other people down? This type of person gets their energy from doing just that. But consider who it is they get their energy from? They are getting it from you. Have you ever noticed the impact this type of person has on you?

The law of resonance started out as a law of physics and states that when two bodies come together, their energy levels converge. The body with the higher energy will lose energy, while the body with the lower energy will gain energy.

For example, let's go back to childhood and play marbles. You ping one marble across the floor at high speed in the direction of a stationary marble. What happens when they collide? The stationary marble starts moving, while the one you pinged continues to move after the collision, but more slowly. In other words, the stationary marble has gained energy, while the fast-moving marble has lost some. Their energy levels are closer together after they've met, the law of resonance in action.

It is the same with human beings. Imagine you're the life and soul of the party, full of energy, and enthusiasm. Then you're made to sit down and talk to someone who looks miserable and low energy. What happens? You will leave that conversation feeling less enthusiastic than before, and your energy will be lower. The other person might have some of your enthusiasm rub off on them and feel a bit better than before. In other words, they gain energy at your expense.

Let's take another example. You spend your whole afternoon in the office with a selection of pessimists, and they have nothing positive to say. How good would you feel by the end of the afternoon? What happens if you're in a meeting, and people do nothing but moan? When people attend meetings like this, the most likely thing that happens afterward is what, exactly? Well, they go talk to someone else who wasn't at the meeting, and moan to them about how bad the meeting was! I make this point to illustrate how easy it is for energy to be drained away. It's easy to take the moaning on board and pass it on to other people. In effect, your energy level dropped to a similar level as other people in that first meeting, and your resultant low energy leads to you complaining about what happened.

The law of resonance applies in reverse too. If you spend more time with optimistic, upbeat people, you are more likely to gain energy and feel better. There are steps you can take to raise your level of energy yourself. But for the moment, let's just compare your energy levels to other people in different situations. Bear in mind that the law of resonance is always working. Your energy and power will be influenced by other people.

One inescapable conclusion from the law of resonance is this; it's almost impossible to stay high energy and powerful if you spend your entire life with negative people. It was Susan Jeffers who pointed this out when she said that you should surround yourself with positive, upbeat people when making changes in your life. To borrow her words, "there is a lightness about positive people. They have learned not to take themselves so seriously and they are a joy to be around."[2] By contrast, one of my colleagues describes the serial energy killer as a *mood hoover*. Mood hoovers suck up all the positive energy in a room with their negativity about this, that, and whatever. If you want to feel good, it's time to vacuum the mood hoovers out of your life or at least confine them to a cupboard where they do less harm!

It is worth considering whom it is you spend your time with; this is our next step.

Exercise: Builders and Demolishers

The steps to follow in completing the exercise are as follows.

Step 1. Make a list of people who you spend time with. They could be work colleagues, family, friends, or other people. Include those people who significantly impact on you, whether at work or elsewhere.

Step 2. Now give each person you have named a score of 1, 2, or 3, according to the following scale:
  ○ Mark 1 against those people who generally leave you feeling better than you felt before you talked to them.
  ○ Mark 2 against those people who either have no appreciable impact on your moods when you meet them or who sometimes leave you feeling better and sometimes worse.
  ○ Mark 3 against those who generally leave you feeling worse than before you talked to them.

Step 3. How many of each category do you have? Are you surrounded by optimists? Pessimists? A mixture?

Step 4. What can you do to increase your exposure to optimists in future? Write down a few options here.

Step 5. Now consider what impact you have on others. Do you raise or lower the energy of other people when you encounter them? Comment on your impact on the people you meet. Of course, you can always ask them if you're not sure and if you're prepared to hear the answer!

Summary

In this chapter, we have explored the second principle of ethical power, which is to notice how you feel in the moment. This will give you helpful information on the state of your power. Noticing how you use your time, and what you focus on, will help here.

You considered some of the telltale signs that indicate that you are losing power. In addition, you thought about the impact of people around you on your power as well as your impact on other people.

Identifying how you hold or lose power is an essential step toward becoming a more ethically powerful person. In the next chapter, we will look at how our power can become derailed and what to do about it.

PART 2

Harnessing Your Energy

CHAPTER 5

Power Trips

Security is mostly a superstition. Avoiding danger is no safer in the long run than outright exposure. Life is either a daring adventure, or nothing.
—Helen Keller

The third step to ethical power—Identify what trips your power switch

The third step to ethical power is to identify the things that trip your power switch. Work out the situations where you allow others to take your power, or where you disable yourself. Become aware of your own natural response to power, including the childhood responses of fight, flight, and freeze. We take our child response into adulthood, and this can trip us up sometimes. Tackling our negative self-talk is important.

Introduction: Our Trip Switches

We've looked at how power is inevitable, that other people can help or hinder your power, and that noticing your moods and emotions is one key to working out what's happening to your power. Things get more complex now because sometimes we can trip ourselves up. We can behave a bit like a power, or electric, circuit. Sometimes we can short circuit ourselves and short out. Or the fuse might blow. Or something else stops the electrical current from flowing; like a resistor, for example. The analogy means that we have our own short circuits and ways of resisting things, and sometimes they can get in our way. When they do, our own power suffers. We've already seen this in some of the moods we've talked about, like our sense of dread. When we approach something with a sense of dread, we are already well on the road to tripping ourselves up.

No matter how powerful we may be, there will be occasions when our power switch trips, we lose power and become less effective. The third step to ethical power is about working out the causes of these power trips when they happen. Once we've worked out the cause, we have a chance to do something about it.

Our personal power can *short out* when faced by particular people or in specific situations. Sometimes the person or situation can cause us to trip. But on other occasions, we can trip ourselves before we even get to the situation in question. For example, I might have a real problem in my head with doing business presentations. Faced with doing a presentation to a group of senior managers, I might worry, fret, and beat myself up so much that I've blown any chance of success before I turn up to do it. It's almost like scoring an own goal or giving away a safety.

The challenge we have is to locate our own individual trip switches when it comes to power. Let's imagine we are sitting in front of a huge river. The water is deep, and the channel the river has been running through has been deepened and worn over many thousands of years. How easy would you say it is to change the direction the river flows in? Short of building a dam, the answer is *not easy*.

So changing our trip switches is not an overnight job. They can be worked on, but it will take time. As a start, just working out what they are will help to tackle them. They arise from the way we live life, from the moment we are born. We announce our arrival in this world by taking in a deep breath and screaming our lungs out. We don't have any power problems at that stage when we make all that noise. We are born without any power switches; a new born baby will be full on. It's not long after this that we develop switches though.

Much of our behavior in relation to power comes from early childhood. It stems fundamentally from two key sources.

1. What do we do when we are under threat?
2. How do we get what we want?

There are four types of power switches that come into play as we grow older, and these types are essentially about answering one of the two questions above. Here, we'll consider each of them in turn. First, they are the primitive animal response we all have of fight, flight, or freeze when faced with a situation we perceive as threatening. Second, the ways that we learn to resist things, situations, and people that we do not want, including change. Third, the beliefs we acquire about *how things are* as we grow up, particularly those beliefs that hold us back. Finally, there's our need for security and the impact of this on our personal power. Let's examine first the most primeval one: How we respond when under threat.

How Power Trips: Fight, Flight, and Freeze

The fight–flight–freeze response was first described by Walter Bradford Cannon in 1929.[1] It kicks in directly in response to the question *what do we do when we feel under threat?* To illustrate this, let's consider what would be an obvious threat to us.

Let's say a tiger comes running by and passes close to you. You essentially have three instinctive reactions in response. You might fight, perhaps by picking up a stick (it being unadvisable to fight unarmed!). Alternatively, you could flee by running away. Your third option is to freeze, either out of terror or in the hope that by staying still you won't be seen or at least seen as a potential meal. These three options are the classic ones of fight, flight, and freeze. When we perceive any sort of threat, our personal power is directly challenged. In childhood, our responses to threat are rather primeval—we will fight, take flight, or freeze (Figure 5.1).

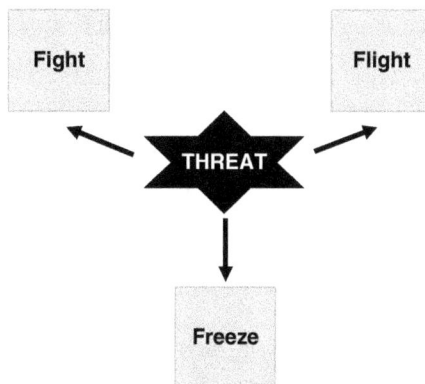

Figure 5.1 Fight–flight–freeze

(Cannon, 1929)

To take this idea further, let's say that as a child you are walking to school one day, and you see someone that you recognize as a bully. You have three basic choices:

1. You can fight them or otherwise make it clear through your talk that you're prepared to stand up to them.
2. You can run away and hope to outrun them.
3. You can freeze, perhaps crouch down, hoping they won't see you.

Your reactions are like those played out in the animal kingdom when faced with a potential threat or predator.

As a child, you may have defaulted to one of these options in threatening situations. If so, you may well have carried this preference into adulthood. By now, the nature of the things that you see as *threats* would have changed. Unless you're very unlucky, you're unlikely to risk being beaten up by the equivalent of the school bully (though some people are unfortunately unlucky). But there will still be *symbolic* threats for you to deal with as an adult. Let's consider one such possible threat as an example.

You're sitting in a business meeting. Two of your colleagues start to argue publicly, and you feel threatened by it. Your choices of what to do here might be:

1. Argue back and get stuck in (fight).
2. Stay compliant or back down to keep the peace (flight).
3. Stay out of the argument, hoping no one will bring you into it (freeze).

Now, you might try to rationally resolve the issue. However, if the threat is significant to you, and your power trips as a result, then you are likely to default to your preferred fight, flight, or freeze option. So, for example, if you know a work meeting is likely to be personally threatening, you might book a holiday to avoid the need to attend (booking a flight; literally a flight response in this case!)

In our early days on this planet, we learn our responses, and these will tend toward one of the three options. As we move into adulthood and our working career, these primeval responses become more refined.

Rather than fight, we may choose to rebel, confront someone, or argue against something. We see this in people always taking on the authorities on whatever issue.

Instead of flight, we may choose to comply, avoid someone, change the subject, or move away. Deference to more senior or powerful people is suggestive of someone who has a strong *flight* response. We may just go along with things even if we have personal reservations about what's going on.

Instead of freezing, we might ignore something in the hope that it goes away.

If our power trips, our instinctive default reaction becomes what we do when faced with a power situation.

- Fight = rebel or confront
- Flight = comply
- Freeze = ignore

What do you tend to do when faced with a threat? Here is an exercise, with some questions to help you work it out.

Exercise: Fight, Flight, and Freeze

1. Think of a situation in your childhood, where you felt in some way under threat. Describe the situation.
2. Now describe how you reacted in the situation. Was it an example of fight, flight, or freeze?
3. Now think of an example from your working life where you felt under threat and you responded with the same strategy as the one you've just described. So, for example, if you responded with a flight reaction as a child, think of an example from the workplace where you did the same.
4. Finally, considering your overall response to threats, which instinctive reaction is your most likely one nowadays—fight, flight, or freeze? What would people who know you well say about you?

ॐ

None of these three options is better than the others. But they all present us with a problem; our instinctive option kicks in when we perceive a threat, often from someone we see as more powerful than us. It is our reaction to power, it's not us empowering ourselves. If you are always reacting to authority in this way, you will never be in authority in your own life.

The fight–flight–freeze options come into play when we're put on the spot in a situation. But let's take this a bit further, because as adults we can become quite sophisticated in disguising what's really going on for us. One element of this is the way we can choose to resist those we see as holding more power. We all have our own ways of resisting others. Let's look at these ways of resisting in more detail. To help with this, I'm going to bring in a sci-fi analogy.

How Power Trips: Our Resistance

As with fight–flight–freeze, the ways that we resist other people and change are deployed when we feel under threat. Those among you who watched *Star Trek*, of the Patrick Stewart hue, will be familiar with that brilliant catchphrase of the human–machine race of conquerors, the Borg. They went into battle with the phrase *resistance is futile, you will be assimilated.* If it hadn't been for Patrick Stewart, they would undoubtedly have won!

Is resistance always a bad thing? Perhaps not, as if we simply went along with everything that hit us, we would soon become amorphous blobs, with no shape to speak of. So, in one respect, resistance has its uses. However, resistance has two drawbacks. First, it is reactive in nature; simply being *against* something says nothing about what it is we are *for.* Second, we often resist unconsciously or subconsciously, while believing that what we're doing is more constructive.

Why Do We Resist?

Fundamentally, we resist other people when we feel under threat or vulnerable. In turn, most of us feel vulnerable either when our security is under threat or when we think we have no control over a situation. If we feel insecure and have no control, we are not in an empowered position and end up wanting to resist whatever or whoever is causing our woes.

Of course, some people can deal with more insecurity than others, and some people can deal with more loss of control than others can. These people are likely to find fewer situations where their power trips.

Given that we all feel vulnerable at times, we will have our own ways of resisting others. The question is, what are our own preferred ways of resisting? Figure 5.2 summarizes the main ones, which we'll go on to examine. It is based on the work of Peter Block,[2] an American author and business consultant, who described what he saw as *the faces of resistance*.

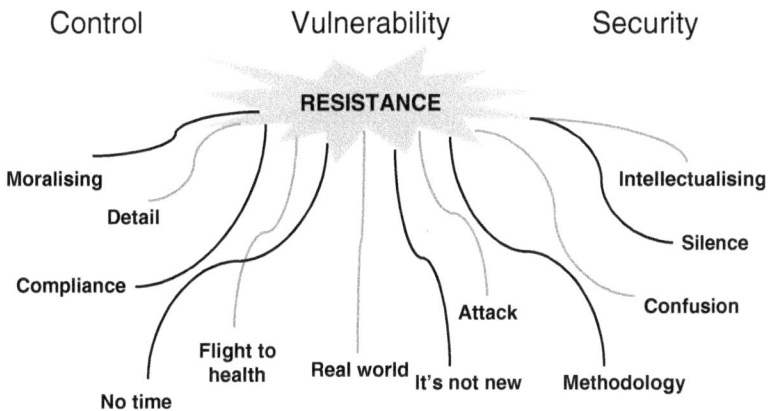

Figure 5.2 Resistance strategies

So what is it we do when we use each of these resistance approaches? It's sometimes difficult to see them in ourselves, but it is certainly easier to see them in other people! Our closest colleagues are more likely to see what we get up to. Let's say a little about each of the resistance strategies mentioned earlier.

Moralizing

Here, we moralize about the situation in question. However, behind this is a classic blame shifting or deflecting attention mentality. "Of course, I understand what needs to be done, but they don't!" Or "if it wasn't for that lot, we wouldn't need to do this." Moralizing is an adult version of the childhood *he said, she said* blaming game.

Detail

With this one, we resort to either requesting more and more information or feeling the need to provide more and more information to someone else. Either way, it is a great delaying tactic to prevent action from being taken.

> I see that change could be good. However, I need more information first, just to be sure.

or

> Before you come to your conclusion, there's more information I need to give you.

This is a great way to procrastinate, rather than address the real issue.

Compliance

I'll go along with it. However, going along with something is not the same as agreeing with it. If it all goes wrong later, I'm not really committed to ensuring that things work out. I may even claim later that I never supported the original idea! Compliance is a low-energy option when we want to resist; I'm neither resisting more actively nor supporting things.

No Time

There are two variants on this theme. One is that I don't have time for this right now. The other is that now is not the right time: Often with this second approach, the right time will never arrive. By using time as an excuse, we hide our real objections to whatever is going on.

Flight to Health

This option is often seen when we resist change we want, like going on a diet! The closer it gets to the deadline for starting a diet, the more we think to ourselves "well I'm not as overweight as I first thought!" In that way, there isn't an issue that needs to be dealt with.

Real World

"Now this might be a great idea in principle, and maybe I might even like to see it happen. But in the real world, it'll never work!" In this way, we reject feedback from other people because they don't understand our real world. We resist change on grounds of practicality. But, of course, if we really wanted it to happen, we would overcome all these so-called practicalities!

It's Not New

"I've heard this all before! We tried it your way 10 years ago, and it didn't work then! I've survived four recessions in my life, why would I worry about this one?" We are resisting other people by effectively saying that we already know what it is they are trying to tell us. That says nothing about whether what they are trying to tell us has a point to it.

Attack

Here, we resist by attacking the person we think is behind whatever is going on. Of course, it is unlikely that we'd end up literally attacking them. However, our verbal assault often ends up being a classic case of shoot the messenger. Attacking someone else removes the need to discuss the issue being raised—for example, "here I am with so much to do, and you come along with this!"

Methodology

With this style of resistance, you hide behind the need for a methodology or procedure. For example, if someone else wants you to move from position A to position B, you might ask them for a methodology; in other words, "what steps do I need to take to do that?" After all, if you are to move from A to B, then you need to understand precisely what to do and in what order. A methodology is needed. Now, sometimes this request can be genuine. However, where you repeatedly ask for the methodology to be broken down further and further, it proves to be a great delaying tactic to avoid something that you do not want.

Confusion

I am confused. If I need to understand the issue before I can do anything, then what a great cop-out it is to fail to understand it! Children do this brilliantly to get out of things they don't want to do. We put the onus on someone else to educate us or even on ourselves to learn at some point in the future. Until either happens, we cannot adapt to whatever is being requested.

Silence

In this case, you choose to say nothing. Faced with someone proposing to do something, or make a change, you respond with no response or even silence. Keep quiet and hope it goes away is the approach you adopt with this resistance strategy.

Intellectualizing

Oh, the power of rationality! Let's talk about the idea more so we fully understand it, from all the different angles possible. But we'll never actually get around to implementing anything. In the personal development arena, this can manifest itself in someone who reads widely, and still nothing improves. There's always another book to read first.

&)

There you have it, 12 ways in which we can resist things we don't like. It's worth pointing out that, on the face of it, some of these could be a legitimate initial response rather than resistance per se. For example, it might make sense to request more information at first or to point out that something has been tried in the past. However, for much if not most of the time, they are simply resistance strategies that are designed to stop us from talking about the real issues or from moving on. They are our approach to dealing with something or someone we see as more powerful. Consequently, saying what we really think is not viewed as a good idea.

It's time to take another look at these strategies and complete the following reflective exercise.

Exercise: My Resistance Strategies

1. Think about a change from the past that you didn't want to happen. Which of the above 12 resistance strategies did you use? How often and at what stages?
2. Thinking more generally, which of the resistance strategies come most naturally to you? If your preferred option doesn't work, where are your back-up options?

℘

One key to managing our own resistance is to start noticing it in the first place. By developing our self-awareness, we will start to notice when our own resistance is kicking in. Once we do notice, we can choose to address the issue in a more open, honest way, rather than hiding behind the resistance option. Later in this book, we will look at how you might address the issue more honestly and assertively if need be.

First, let's look at a couple of case studies to illustrate how resistance can show itself in a real-life situation.

Resistance: Sabotaging Business IT Change

The Situation

You're working away in an office job when your boss shows up and calls a team meeting. She announces that a new computer software system is to be introduced to the team, only 12 months after the last one was implemented. That implementation did not go well and disrupted your work significantly. While your boss extols the virtues of the new system, you suspect that things might not go smoothly. You are also concerned that if this move is successful, the company might need fewer people doing the job you do. Redundancy could be a possibility, and you won't want this.

Your boss has now arranged for a project manager responsible for implementing the new software to talk to each member of the team individually. This includes you. Your conversation goes as follows:

Project manager: I thought I'd talk to each member of the team to see what you thought about the proposed change. Did you have any questions?

You: Not really. I'm confused as to why this software is being
    brought in when the current software is new.

Project manager: Well, this is a major enhancement and will improve
    efficiency in the office by 25 percent.

You: Surely you must have seen this coming. Then why implement
    the last system? You must have known, surely?

Project manager: I wasn't involved in it last time around. However,
    I do know that we were not expecting to make any further
    changes. This software release was not expected when the com-
    mitment was made to go ahead last time.

You: The trouble is you project managers don't plan far ahead. If you
    did my job, you'd know how disruptive this all is. I'm trying to
    service the customer.

Project manager: I realize this will be potentially disruptive, and I'd
    prefer to work with you to minimize the disruption. Once this
    software is in place, it will make your job easier.

You: I heard all this the last time, and it didn't work out that way.

How You Resisted

You started off with the confused option before moving on to the attack.
The project manager was shot as the messenger, even though they weren't
personally involved the last time.

The Outcome

The software was implemented on time, but you never actually clarified
your main concern, which was the fear that there might be job losses
down the line.

An Example of Resistance: Sabotaging Yourself

The Situation

You're a smoker, and for several years at New Year, you've thought about
a resolution to give up smoking. However, this year, you told your spouse
that you were indeed turning over a new leaf, and you are giving up
the weed for good. You're clear on the potential benefits of giving up,

including the health benefits. Not to mention that you'll be spending a lot less and can use the money for better things.

What You Thought

During the run-up to D-day (the day you're due to give up), here are some of the thoughts you had:

> "I've tried to give up before and failed."
> "If it wasn't for these cigarette manufacturers, I wouldn't be smoking at all!"
> "My family all smoke. How am I going to survive in their house?"
> "The trouble with all these 'give up smoking' brigade is that none of them ever had to give up smoking!"

How You Resisted

You started with a version of *I've seen it all before* followed by a sustained bout of moralizing about all sorts of other people including your family.

The Outcome

No real surprise that you failed to give up smoking. Instead, you went into resistance mode rather than working out how to quit smoking and make it work.

∞

We will return to the theme of resistance later in this book, when it comes to how you might handle the resistance you face from other people. But first, we look at another source of power trips; this source kicks in before the event in question. These trips are caused by what we believe, and specifically by disempowering beliefs, or limiting beliefs.

How Power Trips: What We Believe

Where do these beliefs come from? Beliefs come from our experience when younger. They can evolve from the fight, flight, and freeze options when we face threats. However, they also arise from our experience of what to do to get what we want, or to avoid what we don't want. We will grow up believing a variety of positive and negative things, and it is the latter that usually end up tripping our power.

Limiting beliefs often evolve because of bad experiences. We have a bad experience, which colors our view of the future, should a similar situation arise. As with most of the causes of our power trips, limiting beliefs often have their origins in childhood but can develop any time in life. A great example of this is outlined below.

Case Study: Moira

Moira as a child loved the stage. She was outgoing, vibrant, and took part in all the school plays and stage shows and did well for her age. Then there was this one night. She lost part of her outfit before the start of the show. Then she arrived on the wrong part of the stage, partly as she had been trying to find her lost garment. Thrown off balance, she forgot some of her lines and nearly tripped herself up. Finally, someone else appeared on the wrong part of the stage, and Moira gasped with surprise, a move that had some of the audience laughing at her, especially with half her costume still missing.

As a result, Moira lost her confidence on the stage and in front of any audience of more than a few people. The next time she was in public view she didn't do well either. This reinforced her developing view that she was no good on stage in front of lots of people. Gradually, this view strengthened into a belief, *I'm no good in front of people, I'm no good thinking on my feet.* Moira started to avoid situations that might put her in this position; in a manner of speaking, she ran away. Whenever she was forced to do a presentation at work, she froze. In this way, her belief that she was no good became a self-fulfilling prophecy.

For Moira, this had its origin in one bad experience. At the time, rather than saying "I'm good at this, I just had a bad night," she started on the slippery slope to a limiting belief that, when triggered, tripped her power whenever she felt under threat.

The thing about beliefs is they aren't true, but they are self-fulfilling. If you believe something about yourself, the results will probably reinforce the belief. Henry Ford, the founder of the Ford Motor Company, once famously said, "Whether you believe you can do a thing or not, you are right."[3]

We all have loads of beliefs about all sorts of things, ourselves, and other people. Here are just a few:

- I'm no good at selling.
- Strangers are not to be trusted.
- It's rude to say what you want.

These beliefs often stem from our early behavior with those in authority: parents, guardians, teachers, older siblings, and even in some cases friends. From these people, we learn a few tactics or approaches which might get us what we want, as well as avoiding what we don't want. Unpleasant childhood experiences often give rise to negative, or limiting, beliefs. Although the belief may have been useful in the past, it is not serving the person well now in adulthood and in the professional world.

To date, what we've talked about here is stuff we may learn from our parents or other significant people from our childhood. For example, you may have learned to play it safe from someone significant in your life. However, other aspects of our response are learned through other means and sometimes later in life. These later learned responses may trip us up when faced with power.

There are lots of limiting beliefs out there that can shoot our own power in the foot. Just a few examples are given below:

- My memory is awful.
- I'm incapable of doing anything creative.
- If I say what I want, I'll be overruled.
- I should only speak when invited to.
- I have nothing interesting to say.

Beliefs loiter around and then trip us up. The good news is that by identifying where our power trips, we can start to uncover our underlying limiting beliefs. Once we have uncovered them, we can begin to do something about them.

Overcoming a Limiting Belief

Depending on our upbringing and experience, we may have taken on board a range of negative or limiting beliefs that have the effect of holding us back at key times in our professional and personal life. These beliefs, when they come into play, can disable us at certain times or when faced with certain people and situations.

For our purposes, a limiting belief can be defined as follows:

Something your head says to put yourself down, or otherwise limit yourself.

One example of a limiting belief is covered in the following belief cycle (Figure 5.3), taking an individual called Alan.

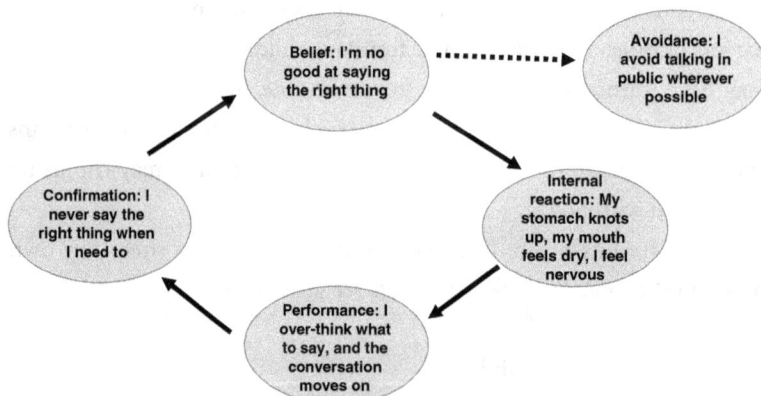

Figure 5.3 Example of a limiting belief

In Alan's case, he has a *belief* that he is no good at saying the right things in public, be it presentations or contributions to meetings he attends. The result is that when faced with a situation where he may need to say something, he experiences some unpleasant *internal reactions*. These are often physical in nature, in this case, linked to nerves about having to say something. In extreme circumstances, Alan might even feel physically sick. Given these reactions, it's no surprise that Alan struggles when he does need to talk. He overthinks what he's going to say. His tendency to overthink means he is still thinking about what to say when other people have moved the conversation on from the bit that Alan heard! As a result, his *performance* suffers. He ends up either saying nothing or making a contribution that no longer reflects the current conversation. This *confirms* Alan's view that he never says the right thing when he needs to, and his existing *belief* is strengthened. If this cycle continues, the likely result is that Alan will attempt to *avoid* any situations where he might need to talk in public. The result is a vicious cycle, or a self-fulfilling prophecy, which trips Alan's power whenever he faces a situation like this. In his current job, this is starting to hold him back; he was recently turned down for a promotion partly because he wasn't seen as having enough *presence* in the team.

It doesn't matter how the belief started. What matters is that it is now a belief, it affects the person's performance when it kicks in, and the results reinforce the belief as in some way true. The belief literally becomes a self-fulfilling prophecy. In the end, if things remain bad enough for long enough, we will go to avoidance behavior. In other words, we will do everything we can to avoid those situations where we feel exposed, in this case by speaking in public.

Now for the good news. A belief can be changed if we work at it. Essentially, we change it by breaking the links that tie the belief cycle together. Taking the above belief as an example, we could start changing it by tackling it at any or all of the following stages:

- Focusing on the *internal reaction* stage, by use of mindfulness exercises (e.g. meditation), or having quiet time before a meeting. You could make sure that you breathe deeply during the meeting; this helps to stay calm.
- Focusing on the *performance* stage by learning to think aloud, so you don't have to get your comments 100 percent right first time. To help here, you might try this at less important meetings first.
- Focus on the *confirmation* stage by asking for feedback on your performance at a meeting: what you did well and what you did less well. This will enable you to gather data on your strengths, allowing you to see a more balanced picture.
- Focus on the *belief* itself through positive affirmations, literally repeating to yourself "I am good in meetings" or focusing on the

aspects of meetings you are good at. So, for example, you might be good at listening and summarizing what other people say. Also, remember meetings that *did* go well for you, so you can say you have been good at meetings in the past.

My main point here is that it is possible to change a limiting belief over time. It won't change overnight, but it will change if you want to change it.

Exercise: My Limiting Belief

I now want you to think about a situation you face (or have faced) where your personal power trips and build up the following belief cycle in your case. Work around the cycle, answering the questions as best as you can.

1. Describe a situation where your power trips.
2. If you are to be faced with a similar situation again, what would your physical symptoms be? In other words, describe your *internal reaction*.
3. What is the *performance*, when you go into the situation you don't want to be in? In other words, what generally happens?
4. What is the result as a rule? What does it *confirm* for you?
5. Sum up what, for you, is the *limiting belief* you must hold to behave like this?
6. To what extent do you now *avoid* these situations completely?

Summarize your thoughts, using a blank version of the following limiting belief cycle (Figure 5.4).

Now consider what steps you could take to break this cycle?

- To control or manage the physical symptoms?
- To improve your performance in the situation next time you face it?
- To challenge your conclusions about what happened?

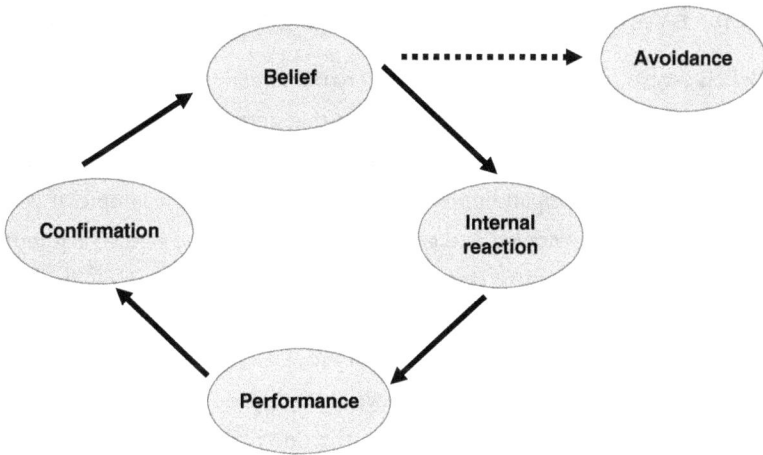

Figure 5.4 My limiting belief cycle

Finally, write down two things you can start doing to deal with this belief and reduce the chances of tripping in future.

ℬ

To illustrate what can happen, Alan overcame the limiting belief he had about his own ability to talk in public, using the techniques to break the cycle referred to above. As a result, Alan now has a much more positive belief about himself (Figure 5.5).

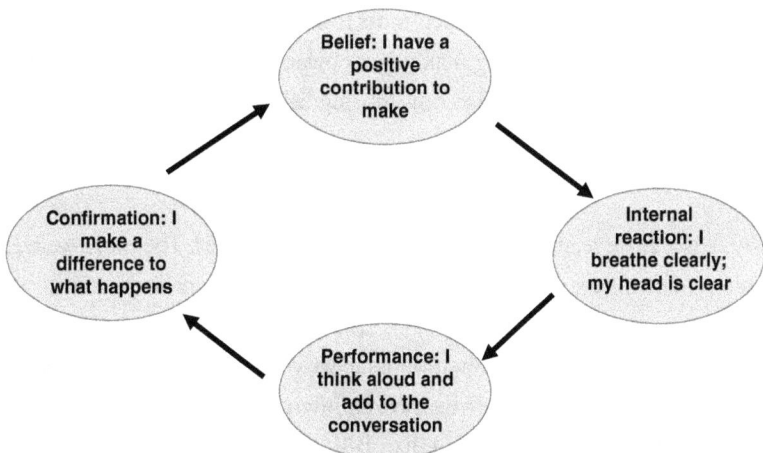

Figure 5.5 Alan's positive belief

The Evolution of Beliefs: Learning versus Ruminating

Beliefs evolve according to how we react to our experience. Limiting beliefs develop from our reactions to experiences that at the time we perceived to be bad experiences. The question is, are these experiences necessarily bad? The answer might depend on our reactions to them. For example, if you put your hand on a cooker and get burnt, the best advice would be to not do it again. But you must clean a saucepan ring sometime. How do you do that unless you put your hand on?

The key is to learn lessons, and then move on, and not get caught up in the drama to the point that you develop a phobia. There is a difference between learning and ruminating. On the one hand, learning is important. It allows us to draw conclusions that will help us to avoid the same fate next time and to improve our performance in the long run. Alternatively, if it's a situation that went well, learning allows us to develop the knowledge, skill, or behavior to ensure we repeat the success and build on it in future. With rumination on the other hand, we don't get over the actual incident. We just replay it in our minds, time and again. You see it in people who don't get over something, ever. Rumination focuses on the pain or trauma and results in avoidance next time. Learning focuses on the lessons and helps to ensure there will be a next time, and it will be a better next time. If you don't allow yourself to make some mistakes, you will never learn anything. Most successful business leaders, for example, will swear blind that they learned most from the times they got it wrong.

In other words, learning maximizes power, whereas rumination ties it up, and develops or reinforces our limiting beliefs.

Our Locus of Control

There is a close relationship between *power* and *control*. The more we feel able to control events, or at least influence them, the more powerful we will feel in return.

The learning versus rumination issue we've just spoken of is linked to our locus of control, whether we have an internal or external locus of control. This work emanates from Julian B Rotter, and it contrasted the two loci we might have.[4] With an internal locus of control, we believe that we can influence the outcomes in our life and that effort will make a difference to the results we achieve, whether in career or in life more generally. With an external locus of control, we are more likely to ascribe the results we achieve as being down to external factors.

The promotion board in the workplace highlights these different approaches, and I have seen both types. Person A, who was unsuccessful, commented that "I didn't prepare as well as I could have, and some of my answers to questions were not as good as I would have liked." Person B's reaction was "I was up against someone whose face fits, so I had little chance of getting the job." Person A has an internal locus, putting the results down primarily to their own efforts (or lack of effort!). Person B has an external locus, putting the result down to factors outside their control.

In this context, learning is more likely to fit with an internal locus of control. Rumination is more likely to be a consequence of an external locus of control (for example, "why does this always happen to me?")

There is researched evidence to suggest that internally driven people will move on more and test their comfort zones more frequently than people who have an external locus of control. For example, one study highlights that internals are more likely to be more influential in the organization they work for, as well as being more likely to change organization in pursuit of a better job than employees with an external locus.[5]

Awareness of Beliefs

I mentioned earlier that a belief won't change overnight. However, that isn't the same as saying that nothing can change quickly. Even becoming aware of our own limiting beliefs will begin the process of changing them, if we want to.

This is illustrated with the help of the conscious competence approach, originally based on a model designed by Gordon Training International.[6] In diagrammatic form, it charts how we move from being not competent at something to being fully competent at it. It takes us through four main stages on the journey (Figure 5.6).

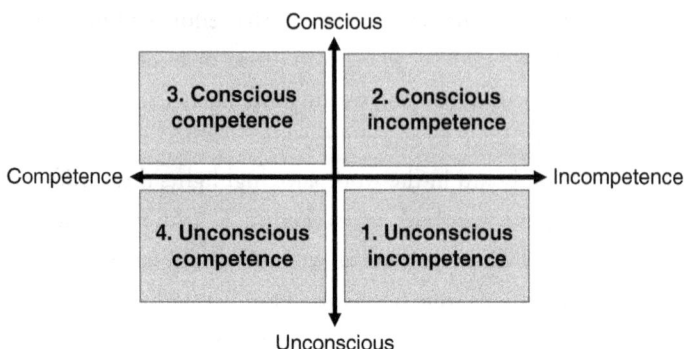

Figure 5.6 *The conscious competence model*

(Adams, 2018)

Stage 1: Unconscious Incompetence

At this stage, I am blithely unaware of my lack of competence. It may be because I've never had to be competent at something, for example driving before the age of 18. In this case, there was little point in trying to become competent, as driving is generally illegal before that age. I have met thousands of people during my career who were utterly convinced that they would be able to do their manager's job better than their manager could! This is a great illustration of unconscious incompetence at work—we don't know what we don't know.

Alternatively, we may just not be very good at something, but not realize this, until someone points it out to us. As a result, I am incompetent, and I am unconscious of the fact. Once I do become aware, we move to Stage 2.

Stage 2: Conscious Incompetence

I am now painfully aware that I lack competence and need to raise my competence level. I have now moved from the Stage 1 "I don't know what I don't know" position to one of "I certainly do know what I don't know!" At Stage 2, the impetus to do something about it gathers momentum. So, to use the driving example, I want to drive, it's now legal, but the first time I step into the driver's seat, I realize all too well how little I know about driving. I am incompetent and conscious of this.

In business, a few of those *thousands of people* I referred to above did get the opportunity through promotion to do their manager's job. Most of them found out pretty quickly that it was not an easy job to do, managing all those staff who thought they could do a better job of it!

Stage 3: Conscious Competence

In this stage, I start raising my skill level. By practicing enough, I improve to the point that I become consciously competent. In any activity, like driving, a beginner gradually becomes consciously competent. This means they can perform the task, like drive the car, but they must think about it as they do it (e.g., mirror, signal, maneuver). I am not able to do the task automatically, but I can do it when I have to.

The newly promoted office manager, through development and some experience, will get to the point where they are able to assess their staff's performance through giving feedback. But they have to think about it before they do it; it isn't something they can do automatically. They may need to put a lot of energy into thinking about the right way to give constructive criticism, for example.

Stage 4: Unconscious Competence

I am now able to do the task unconsciously, without conscious thinking. Most experienced drivers can get into a car and drive it without even thinking about what they need to do. Driving has become second nature. Of course, we must be careful not to let bad habits set in. Otherwise, we may end up in Stage 1 again, unconsciously incompetent at some aspect of driving.

The office manager will also become more comfortable with managing her team and their performance. But again, she needs to watch, in case bad habits set in.

୭

The main point of this model when it comes to our beliefs is that once we become aware of our beliefs about ourselves, we move from Stage 1 to Stage 2. We are now conscious of our incompetent belief, and we realize it is holding us back from achieving what we might achieve. We are now consciously incompetent because of our belief. Once we realize this, we can do something about it.

Another way of looking at Stage 2 is that we are now shining a light on the corruption of our mind that leads to nonproductive beliefs about ourselves. By shining the light in their direction, we bring our belief from unconscious to conscious.

If we think about other types of corruption, for example in business, we realize that it thrives when there is no chance of it being discovered. Corrupt executives are encouraged to be corrupt because they think they can get away with it. If a whistle-blower or the media highlights corrupt practice, that alone will reduce the effect of corruption because the light is shining, and our corrupt executive will watch his conduct. It is the same with our corrupt beliefs. If we become aware of corrupt beliefs, we shine a light on them, and they will start to watch it too. But we need to keep shining the light to do this! Awareness won't change a belief on its own, but it's a very good start. We still must work at it by breaking the limiting belief cycle if we are to move to Stages 3 and 4 of the conscious competence model.

How Power Trips: The Need for Security

Returning to our childhood responses to power at the beginning of this chapter, I mentioned how they were determined by two questions: How do I behave when under threat, and how do I get what I want? The final source of power trips is more of a response to the first question on threats. The answer is focused on retaining a degree of security.

Let's begin with a general point on power trips. If you think of a power trip being like a fuse blowing in a plug, what thoughts come into your mind? Maybe that the fuse could be faulty. There may be something wrong with the electrical appliance that means a leak. There are different types of fuse: 3, 5, and 13 amps, for example.

It's fair to say that people have different capacities before their power trips. Capacities, that is, for uncertainty and certainty. The more you can tolerate uncertainty, the greater your potential power, and the less likely you are to trip. We all have a need for security. Depending on how powerful this need is, we may be willing to try new things to push our comfort zone out a bit. The more we're willing to push it out, the more powerful we can become. Some people will trip before they get anywhere.

Think of the lion in his zoo cage. It has been in that cage ever since it can remember. Then, suddenly the cage door opens. It's unlikely that our lion will leave the cage straightaway. He might look through the open space, move toward the entrance, and will eventually move through it. But he won't go far at first, because it feels strange being outside the cage. Our lion might choose to sit just outside the cage initially, in case he needs to go back in. It'll be a while before he moves far away from the cage. It's the same with us humans. We have our cages too, and it can take time before we leave them behind; and some people may never do so.

However, consider where the caged lion gets his security from? From the cage, not himself! But when he has left the cage, the security he gets comes from knowing he's a lion, that he is powerful, and can look after himself. Which security is the better option, do you think? From knowing he's a lion, of course!

We have our comfort zones, which are like cages. Inside our comfort zone, we feel secure. But when we push against the exit, it can feel uncomfortable, particularly if we haven't done it often in the past. This discomfort, allied with one or two bad experiences, may lead some people to stop trying. The trouble is that it's only when we leave the cage that we stop existing and start living. It's only when we push our comfort zones out, that we get to find out just how powerful we could really be.

Many people set themselves up for living small, protected, secure lives. At the center of this is the desire for a small, protected, secure job. But this comes at the expense of their own power, which is sacrificed in exchange. True security comes from looking after yourself in the world. Besides, the cage is an illusion. After all, we all die one day, so what use is the cage? All the cage represents is a coffin for the undead!

Some people need a huge amount of security. In the workplace, they will expect their manager to have all the answers and to provide them. In a world of change, be it restructuring, product changes, technology, or markets, there will be few if any managers who can provide the answers to all these questions.

On a different note, it is a well-known fact that some prisoners reoffend because they want to return to jail. It's secure, they get a roof over their head, food, and companionship. It literally is their cage and they're comfortable in it, compared to being outside in the big bad world. This is an extreme example of people giving up their power in exchange for security.

What Gives Us Security?

Security was highlighted by Peter Block in his resistance model, illustrated in Figure 5.2, as one of the underlying causes of resistance behavior. It is worth bearing in mind that security will differ from person to person. We look for different things to differing degrees.

David Rock, the director of the NeuroLeadership Institute, identified five domains that we seek to protect in a situation of flux or change, which by implication will threaten our level of security.[7] These five domains are status, certainty, autonomy, relatedness, and fairness; the initials go to make up what has become known as the SCARF model. All of the domains matter. However, for each of us, one or two are likely to be more important than the others, and they drive our social behavior when faced with impending change.

Status

Status is our position in the organizational order, our relative importance compared to other people. It can be our position in the management hierarchy, but not always. For example, I did some consulting work in a retail food business that restructured itself at the team leader level. Previously, team leaders had been specialists in their area, for example bakery, fish, meats, or dry goods. Under the new structure, they had more general across the board responsibilities. I remember that causing a problem for one bakery team leader who struggled to come to terms with no longer having a *baker* status. That had been important to him.

Certainty

We all need at least some certainty in our career and life. We want to know what is happening when and to accurately predict what the future holds. For some people, this translates into a low tolerance for uncertainty. In a business change situation, they will want to know well in advance *exactly* what is going to happen and when. They will want all the detail now. Lack of knowing is a significant source of stress. If you manage someone who has a high need for certainty, expect to be asked lots of questions—including many that you won't be able to answer!

Autonomy

Autonomy is our area of control over events. Having an area of responsibility or discretion where I can make the decisions allows me a degree of security. For someone with a high need for autonomy, the detailed micro-manager will be a significant source of stress! This is one reason why giving staff a say in business change can help engage them to a greater degree—they have some say in at least part of what's going on. Being allowed to get on with the job with minimal interference will be a good thing. There is evidence that employees with high autonomy needs are likely to see self-employment as an attractive option. There is nothing more autonomous than being your own boss!

Relatedness

This is about being safe with other people who are friendly. We all have a need to belong with others, but for some people this is particularly important. For example, in business change situations, their main concerns will be around "whom will I be working with?" and "will they be nice people?" Office moves can be particularly challenging for people with a high need for relatedness.

Fairness

This focuses on whether fair exchanges are taking place between people. Are things being done fairly, or is it all a bit underhand? In a situation of change, this type will challenge the way things are being done, in the hope that decisions will be made according to fair process, and they will be the first to complain if that is not the case!

ഇ

The five domains impact on our level of security or insecurity. Given that we will assign different weights to each domain from other people, it is clear that events that would trip one person might not trip someone else in the same way. In other words, the domains that we seek to protect the most are the ones most likely to trip up our power levels.

Exercise: What Do You Seek to Protect?

To some degree, we all like at least some level of security, of home, job, in our relationships, or even in our views of the world. Which of the SCARF domains potentially leave you most vulnerable?

1. Which of the five domains are most significant to you? Status, certainty, autonomy, relatedness, or fairness?
2. Taking one of your significant domains, think about a situation where you felt that your domain was threatened by someone or something happening?
3. What impact did this event have on your personal power levels?
4. What did you feel like doing in this situation?
5. What did you do in practice? What was the result?

ഇ

As a general principle, when true security comes from within ourselves, rather than through comfort zones and cages, we end up power tripping a lot less and experimenting a lot more. We will handle potential threats to our SCARF domains more productively and less reactively. We then move into government in our business rather than handing that responsibility over to others.

Summary

In this chapter, we have explored the third principle of ethical power, which is to identify the situations and people that trip your power switch, causing you to lose your power. These switches can be triggered by your childhood responses to power (fight, flight, and freeze): by how you resist what's going on, by your negative and limiting beliefs, and by your need for security in life. You have considered the impact of each of these areas in your working life, as well as more generally.

We learn some things from childhood that may help or hinder our approach to power, like complying or rebelling. Some beliefs will get in the way if we let them, particularly if we focus on the pain rather than the lessons. If we work out what trips our power switch, we can begin to do something about it.

Let's return to the river we spoke of earlier. A river in full flow has abundant energy within it. Like that river, we each have abundant energy, and abundant energy creates abundant power, if we let it. The trouble is that our energy and power can be undermined by our blockages, which trip the power switch. Think of these blockages as rocks in the river. Most rivers will contain huge boulders and rocks, which could sink any ship that powers down the river, if they come into contact. In the same way, your rocks can sink your personal power, the desire to avoid conflict, the need for security, and other limiting beliefs you may hold. Figure 5.7 illustrates how this river might look for two different people, Person 1 and Person 2.

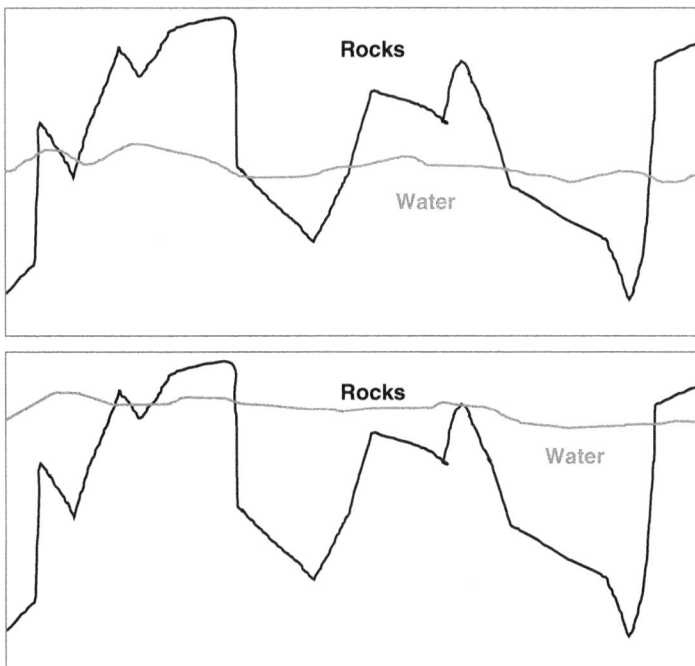

Figure 5.7 River and rocks

One approach you can take to increase your own power is to reduce or remove those rocks that sink your power. That is the approach taken in this third step to ethical power. But could you also do anything to raise your own water level, reducing the effect of the rocks? Can you take steps to raise your own energy levels? In the next chapter, we will consider how we can raise our personal energy levels, so the rocks of our own beliefs and behavior have less effect on us, less often. If we look at Figures 5.6 and 5.7, clearly Person 1 is going to trip up more often than Person 2, as their water level (representing energy) is sufficiently low that rocks will be hit regularly. While Person 2 might have their off moments, they are more likely to be able to literally navigate their way through life without their power tripping. So, our next step to ethical power will be to assess the level of our water.

CHAPTER 6

Your Current Level
of Power

*Though no one can go back and make a brand-new start, anyone can
start from now and make a brand-new ending.*

—Carl Bard

The fourth step to ethical power—Assess your current level of power

The fourth step to ethical power is to assess your current level of power by examining each area of your life. The happier you are with an area of your life, the more empowered you are in that area, and vice versa. The more energy you have overall, the less tired you feel, and the more empowered you are.

It is Wednesday morning, and my boss Andrea calls me into her office for a *chat*. I've worked for Andrea long enough to understand what a chat means. It usually means that she wants to tell me something that she knows I won't want to hear. It might be feedback on something I've done that she or someone else doesn't like and she's going to tell me. It could be a piece of work she wants to dump on me that I won't want. It could be just good old-fashioned bad news. But whatever it is, I don't go into her office expecting to have a good time. As I arrive at her door, I am already dreading what the next 5 minutes will bring, and I hope it will be only 5 minutes.

I knock at her door and go in. I sit down at her invitation. *Oh, good morning Martin.* She says this almost as if she didn't expect it to be

(*Continued*)

me, even though she arranged the meeting and I'm generally on time. This is followed by *how's your morning going?* This gets the now usual reply of *fine*, followed by some inane comment of mine on a topic I'm dealing with that is not too controversial. If I ever have controversy, I'd save it for later, as Andrea never expects a long reply to her greeting.

The next stage of our conversation is the *scene set*, a favored tactic of the manager. They are trained to always set out the big picture or context for whatever it is they are going to do to you. I know this, of course, for two reasons. First, because I've been a victim often enough to recognize the signals. Second, because I'm a manager too and have been on management development courses that tell me this is important. The scene set this time is interesting, sort of.

"You know Martin that I'm due to attend a conference next week in London, on 'Strategic Regulation in the Twenty Twenties.' It's looking at how financial services companies like ours might best regulate ourselves in the next 10 to 15 years, given the changes in the global economy."

I immediately thought about all these changes. Pension crises, banking collapses, economic recession, currency crises, the European Union, all the controversies surrounding the running of companies like ours, and the low esteem in which we are now held by the public.

As I thought about all this, I nearly missed the next bit.

"Unfortunately, Martin, I've been called away next week for personal reasons, and it's imperative that we are represented on the conference and that we are seen to be there. It would be an enormous favor to me if you would agree to attend in my place. We can talk before then about your role there, and what you might say, if that would help."

Not good news! This is short notice; I've got social arrangements set up next week, and the rest of my work priorities will be sidelined. Besides, Rachel will be mad. She never likes it when I'm away anyway, and I've been away quite a bit recently. Only 2 weeks ago, I placated her on my return from a trip to Paris by saying that it was the last time for a while (and usually my trips away are planned well ahead). This gap is not a while, and I can expect an argument at home. These thoughts raced through my head.

"Well, I'll need to look at my priorities," I said, while Andrea looked at me with searching eyes. She also remained silent. My next words were "and I'm sure I can do something." Now I could technically say that I didn't say yes, but that was just a technicality. I'd just said yes. I knew it, and Andrea knew I knew it.

The deal was done. The hurricane would follow. London would probably come as a relief after that.

Some of the above account might be amusing. However, Martin has some significant challenges and tensions in his life. His relationship with Andrea for a start. Then relations with his wife Rachel look challenging too. All this combined with his social life and other work priorities help to paint a picture of someone *out of power* in certain respects. All of which leads on to the next step to ethical power.

Introduction: My Current Power Levels

The fourth step to ethical power has some common ground with the second, in that it draws a comparison between how you feel and your state of power. However, there is one main difference. The second step comprises a snapshot of your feelings in the moment, based on the situation you are in at the time. The fourth step is more of a survey across the whole of your life. It is more of a comprehensive review of your power.

With Step 4, the core premise is that the happier you are with an area of your life, the more empowered you are likely to be in it. Similarly, the less happy you are, the lower your level of empowerment is likely to be. This is common sense, given that most people would not choose to be unhappy or discontented. So, if you are unhappy, then it implies that you do not have sufficient influence over that area. If that is the case, something needs to be done by you.

Returning to the discussion on our locus of control from the last chapter, this step to ethical power is likely to be particularly useful if we ourselves hold an internal locus of control. In other words, we see the results we achieve as largely down to our own efforts. By implication, if we want to improve the results, we can do this by changing what we do. If we hold an external locus of control, we see the results as being beyond our control, perhaps primarily the result of luck or personal circumstances.[1]

The next step then is to diagnose your relationship with power. The following exercise will give you the opportunity to assess your state of power in different areas of your life as well as across your whole life. This is an exercise I have designed for use with my coaching clients when self-empowerment is an issue.

Exercise: How Empowered Am I Right Now?

Ideally, you should complete this exercise three times if you can, taking a different segment of your life for each attempt. The three segments I'd like you to take are:

1. *Your family*—that is your immediate family, parents, spouse or partner, and children.
2. *Your job, career, or vocation*—usually whatever it is that you spend most of your time doing. For most of you, that will be a job, or possibly studying.
3. *Your other relationships*—that includes your wider family, friends, and other important relationships in your life.

Table 6.1 lists 20 paired statements that I want you to consider: *A* and *B*. For each pair, you are to choose the statement that is closer to how you feel about your state of power in each of the three areas above. *A* illustrates an empowered state, while *B* illustrates the disempowered state.

Table 6.1 How empowered am I?

	Category A	Category B
1.	I can do what I want.	I am prevented by others from doing what I want.
2.	I can act on my own when I need to do anything.	I need permission from others to act before I do anything.
3.	I can speak my mind.	I must guard what I really think.
4.	I set my own goals in this area.	Other people set my goals for me.
5.	I feel contented with my life in this area.	I feel discontented with my life in this area.
6.	I gain energy when I'm operating in this area.	I lose energy when I operate here; I feel energy draining away.
7.	I have control of my life in this area.	I feel like other people control my destiny.
8.	I am surrounded by optimistic people.	I am surrounded by pessimists, who drain me.
9.	The things that matter to me are going well.	Things are not going well.
10.	I'm able to operate in line with my own personal principles.	I'm often told to act against these principles and do so.
11.	I feel able to articulate my own needs.	I'm unable to articulate them most of the time.
12.	I look forward to my dealings with people/activities.	I don't look forward to it, or them.
13.	I can get my message across to others.	I'm not able to get my message across.
14.	I feel confident in this area.	I lack confidence in this area.
15.	I feel able to make choices that matter to me.	The choices are not mine to make.
16.	I have access to all the information I need.	I'm kept in the dark on what's really going on.
17.	I feel involved and able to participate.	I feel marginalized in this area.
18.	My rights are respected by other people.	My rights are overridden by other people.
19.	I allow others to express themselves, without my feeling defensive.	I feel defensive when others express themselves.
20.	I get on with the *here and now*.	I am preoccupied with things that happened in the past or might happen in future.

Scoring the Questionnaire

Once you have completed the questionnaire each time, simply score the questionnaire for each area by:

1. Adding up the total number of As and Bs.
2. Subtract the B score from the A score.

The result gives you an empowerment score for that area.

This final score could be either positive or negative. The lowest score is −20, and the highest score is +20. Which of the categories below did your score fall within?

1. If you scored +10 or more: Congratulations, you appear to be reasonably empowered in this category. The closer to 20 your score is, the more empowered you are. In this case, why are you reading this book? Perhaps you are curious or interested in helping other people, but you don't see much further need to help yourself, at least in this area of your life.
2. +5 to +9: You have some influence over this area, but not to the degree you might want. It may be worth looking to see whether there are any themes to the areas where you feel disempowered. The scores suggest that you have some issues with power. However, these issues haven't affected your whole life in this area. Perhaps they are only issues at certain times or with certain people. If you could sort these out, you would feel a whole lot better.
3. −5 to +4: You are significantly lacking in power in this area. What goes on in your life here is seriously challenging your levels of power to achieve things. You have work to do to raise your power levels, and the approaches outlined in the rest of this book will help you with this.
4. −20 to −6: You are basically a passenger in this part of your life, and life will not feel like your own. You need urgently to act to raise your personal power levels. If you're scoring this low in one category, it's likely that you have issues with power across the whole of your life.

℘

Taking your results, now consider your answers to the following reflective question: What three specific things could you do to increase your sense of empowerment in your career and in your life? This could be any of the following or other actions you think appropriate:

- Talk to certain people.
- Work on some of your own beliefs that hold you back.
- Act differently when you're faced with certain types of situation.

My Current Power Reality

Don't get too down on the results if you ended up in category four with your score. At least you are probably being honest with yourself. Your scores will to some degree reflect your mood when you completed the questionnaire. However, the results give you an initial impression of the different parts of your life, and where you can improve it. Whether you have challenges in specific areas of your life or across whole of life, there are steps we can take to raise our power levels.

One client's reaction on completing this exercise was as follows:

"Well, I've done my homework, my life review. Tells me my life's in a mess. I've been thinking all day, good thoughts, some not as good. I have a range of emotions, some hopeful, some scary."

Another reaction was:

"I've complied with my family, at times with my husband, with my career. Anyone looking at me from the outside would see that I'm Mrs. Conventional, living my timetabled life in the same way as all the other Mr. and Mrs. Conventional's. All of us in our own boxes. I found myself wondering where in my life I'd made the decision that cost me a lot. Or was it a succession of small decisions, or more likely nondecisions, that cost me over a period of time."

Both are stark reactions, but stark reactions often result in action. That is the value of Step 4.

The Value of Mindset

Our state of mind is crucial to how effectively we will complete this exercise—and by *effectively*, I mean how honest we will be in completing it. For one thing, if we adopt an external locus of control, we will probably have been making our own excuses for the answers we gave in the above questionnaire. Our thought process will be along the lines of "I may have become disempowered in such and such an area, but that's only because of . . ." We will be making fewer excuses if we have an internal locus of control (e.g., "I see how I've brought this about").

Carole Dweck, as a result of research into student learning,[2] identified two contrasting mindsets we might have concerning our ability or talent to accomplish a task. We can take a *fixed mindset* view, where we see our ability or talent as essentially a fixed property to be proved. Alternatively, we may adopt a *growth mindset*, where we view our ability or talent as more flexible—we can improve our performance (as opposed to simply proving our level) through hard work and learning lessons. With a growth mindset, talent and ability are simply our starting point.

We see fixed mindsets all around us. The person who says "I'll never be any good at presentations" is adopting a fixed mindset. With a growth mindset, we might say "my last presentation could have been better. But if I learn from it, and work hard next time, I can do better." With a fixed mindset, we avoid examining our failures; why bother when I can't improve anyway? With a growth mindset, we will be drawn to our own past failings as a starting point for self-improvement.

Adopting a growth mindset isn't easy. However, it is essential if we are to look honestly at our current performance with a view to improving things. A growth mindset will help us to realize that, until we are honest with ourselves about our shortcomings (which may have been revealed by the questionnaire we have just completed), we won't be able to lay the foundations for our future improvement and empowerment.

Summary

In this chapter, we have explored the fourth principle of ethical power, which is to assess your current level of power across your life by carrying out a power audit. This will give you an overall view of your state of power. You have carried out an exercise to audit yourself and to identify some actions you want to take. We have also compared alternative states of mind that will help us to make the best use of our self-audit to provide the foundations for future improvement.

Before we move on to the fifth principle in the next chapter, let's recap where we have got to in our ethical power journey. Steps 2–4 were all steps that involved diagnosing where we currently are with power. Step 2 looked at how we feel at a moment in time. Step 3 focused on spotting those times when our power trips and starting to identify some of the causes of this. Step 4 took more of a whole life approach, gathering evidence on our state of power in each key area of our life.

In the Power = Energy × Application formula I described in the introduction to this book, we have now explored the *Power* element thoroughly and diagnosed our existing levels of *Energy*. In raising our own energy levels, the next step is to work out where you want to go, and this is the territory of Step 5. We move beyond diagnosis to direction. In the next few chapters, we turn to this biggest of questions; where is it that we would choose to use our power to go?

CHAPTER 7

What Matters?

Our greatest fear should not be of failure, but of succeeding at things in life that don't really matter.

—Francis Chan

The fifth step to ethical power—Get clear on what matters

The fifth step to ethical power is to get clear on what matters. Decide what's really important to you, your own purpose and personal values. Being clear about these tells us where we need to exert our personal power. If we have no clear sense of direction, we will always be reacting to other people's agendas rather than setting our own.

Introduction: Getting Direction

The biggest lesson I've learned in my life is to follow my heart, not my head. This lesson has had significant impact over both my working career and wider life. Use your heart to decide what to do, and then use your head to work out how to get there. Don't use your head to work out what to do, or you'll never change anything, because there will always be reasons why it won't work out.

This is easier said than done. How do we make sure our heart makes the big decisions? The fifth step to ethical power will show you how to do this. This step is about getting clear on what really matters to you in your work and life, allowing you to make informed choices on where to empower yourself. Just how do you become clear? The answer to this comes in two parts: clarity on your own purpose and clarity about your own personal values. The formula for Step 5 to ethical power boils down to a simple equation, which is:

$$Direction = purpose + values$$

Why Direction Matters

In the modern era, gaining a sense of direction matters more than ever before. Just consider how things work nowadays. We have global TV news, with its never-ending emphasis on crisis, war, and bad news. We have reality TV, which is based on anything but reality. We have computer games that are so sophisticated that you almost need a degree to play them. You can certainly spend half your life building your skill levels and expertise in playing games. For most of us, of course, we have work and what often goes with it, long hours. *Too much work, not enough time for life* seems to be the prevailing cry.

Work is long, and life is full of diversions to take our attention away from the one thing that matters most: our sense that we are doing something worthwhile. If only we'd stop and listen, to notice what's going on. To think about what's important to us. That's what this chapter is about: getting to the root of what we're about in an era that isn't favorable to us finding it. We can be a hero in that computer game, or we can be a hero in our real life. Which would be better, do you think?

Without a sense of direction, we will end up drifting through our careers and through life more generally. Some people will drift aimlessly, while others will drift despite appearing to be busy doing and achieving lots of things. It will only ever be an appearance because one day that person will wake up and wonder *why am I doing this?* To answer the question of why, it is vital to get a good handle on what matters to you; clarity on your purpose and values is important. Let's look at each of them in turn.

Your Purpose

What is your purpose? In an earlier chapter, we used the analogy of a river. Let's return to that analogy. What is a river's purpose? Why is it doing what it's doing? The answer is, of course, it is flowing out to the sea. The river's purpose is to flow out to the sea. Everything the river does is with that intention. Now I know the river isn't a life form, but let's say it had no purpose or sense of direction. There would be no current, no waves, no flow of water, and no movement at all. It is the river's purpose that gives it energy to flow in one direction and not the other and toward a specific destination.

Identifying your purpose is important to give you focus. Your purpose could be seen as the bit of the horizon you want to aim for. That will give you the overall direction against which you can assess your progress. Besides, if you don't know where you stand, there will be no shortage of people to tell you.

Your purpose is sometimes not easy to work out, but some questions that might help to identify it include the following:

- What are you passionate about?
- Where is it that you make a difference, or have unique skills? What are you naturally good at?
- What activities, when you do them, cause you to lose all track of time; for example, because you enjoy doing them?
- What do other people say you should have done for a career?
- When you were a child, what was it you said you wanted to do, or be? Think about why that was; what was the appeal?
- If you could get paid for doing your favorite thing, what would you be doing?

As you answer these questions, you might find that things become clearer and that patterns start to emerge in the answers. From this, you would eventually arrive at a short summary of your purpose.

Let me illustrate how these questions might help you to identify your life purpose, using a couple of case studies.

Case Study: David

David answered the questions in the following way, thinking about his career.

"When I thought about the unique skills question, one of mine has always been my ability to get people to open up and talk to me. I naturally attract people who want to talk, and even as a child I was great at getting other kids to talk to me.

Then going to another question, I wanted to be a lighthouse keeper when I was about 6 years old. That might sound antisocial, but

(Continued)

I thought back to what it was about being a lighthouse keeper that I liked the idea of at that age. After all, I didn't know anything about the job then. That made it an emotional decision, not a rational one. I realized that what attracted me was the idea of shining a light to help others to avoid danger and get to where they wanted to go.

Then if I think about when I lose all track of time, it's when I'm talking and listening to people, usually with only one or two people at a time. I gradually realized that my purpose was to help other people to find their way to where they want to get to, by listening to them and giving helpful advice."

Do you get the idea of how to clarify your purpose?

Case Study: Heather

Heather came up with the following answers to the above questions:

What is it in life I am passionate about?
I am passionate about lots of things. Justice, fairness, and helping others are all important to me. Wanting things to be done fairly for everyone.

Where is it that I make a difference or have unique skills? What am I naturally good at?
I have a good sense of humor. It is important to see the funny side of things and not take events too seriously.

What am I naturally good at?
Knowledge of history. I like history because it's important to learn lessons from the past, so we can avoid making the same mistakes in future. In addition, it's important that previous injustices are not forgotten by the next generation.
I am good at reading people and enquiring into things. I like people watching for this reason, and I like to work out what makes them tick.
I am great at analyzing all sorts of things, from spreadsheets, to people's motives, to sports statistics!

What activities, when I do them, cause me to lose all track of time; for example, because I enjoy doing them?
Learning new things, talking to people, and people watching. I also love the countryside and nature.

What do other people say I should have done for a career?
My mum thought I should have been an historian. My husband says I should be a chat show host.

When I was a child, what was it I said I wanted to do or be? Think about why that was; what was the appeal?
I wanted to be a rugby referee! Then I could make sure the game was played fairly, and the decisions made were always right. Plus, I could get to see games for free!

If I could get paid for doing my favorite thing, what would I be doing?
Highlighting wrongdoing and injustice wherever I see it and helping the victims.

Based on her patterns in the above answers, Heather noticed the following:

There's something about justice, fairness, and helping others. Learning lessons from the past and talking to people. I want to highlight injustice in a public way and help other people to deal with the results.

She moved on to summarize her purpose as:

My purpose is to promote justice and fairness and to publicly highlight their breach so that it doesn't happen again, and everyone learns from it.

She felt strongly having completed this exercise that this is what she was here to do.

Exercise: Find Your Own Purpose

This is your opportunity to work through the questions we've just talked about and answer them for yourself. They are designed to help you clarify different aspects of what your purpose might be. As a reminder, these questions are:

1. What are you passionate about?
2. Where is it that you make a difference or have unique skills? What are you naturally good at?
3. What activities, when you do them, cause you to lose all track of time; for example, because you enjoy doing them?
4. What do other people say you should have done for a career?
5. When you were a child, what was it you said you wanted to do, or be? Think about why that was; what was the appeal?
6. If you could get paid for doing your favorite thing, what would you be doing?

୫୨

Having completed your answers, read through them again. What patterns do you notice in the answers you have given to the above questions?

Finally, try to summarize what you think your career or life purpose is in no more than two sentences.

Purpose and Power

As mentioned earlier, your purpose is that part of the horizon you want to aim for, where you want to go in life. One obvious point is to focus your power on getting to that place. This will give you momentum in the same way that a river has momentum. Otherwise, the risk is you just end up drifting. If you know your direction and focus your power on getting there, it will be more obvious to you who is helping you and who isn't.

As we will go on to see, it is important to choose your battles. Your power may be blocked, drained, undermined, and stopped at many times and places. It may be done intentionally or completely by accident. Most people don't set out to deliberately undermine each other, but it still happens. In organizations, with their politics, different power plays will also be made. Being clear about your purpose will help you to choose when it matters, and when it matters less. When it matters, you can then take steps to empower yourself.

Your Personal Values

Your personal values are also important to you when it comes to power. These values are the principles by which we live. Often, we expect others to adhere to the same principles. Whether we are aware of them or not, our values often make themselves known most forcefully when they are violated by ourselves or by other people.

If our purpose is the part of the horizon we are aiming to reach, our personal values are the compass we use to navigate our way through life.

One good way to begin to identify your own values is to think of people you admire in life, and what makes you admire them. This will tell you something about what you value.

To take an example, I'm an admirer of the late Nelson Mandela. I admired his belief in humanity, and his incurable optimism about the future and about human nature. He had this despite losing 30 years of his life to imprisonment by a cruel racist regime that viewed him as little better than an animal. He lost the best years of his life to captivity. Did that leave him embittered? Not a bit of it. Instead, he embraced his captors on release from prison and built bridges with the white community when he took power in South Africa. He chose to see the good in other people.

I learned from him that I have a value around optimism; seeing the good in other things and other people. I expect things to turn out for the best and see the glass as half full rather than half empty. You will not be surprised to hear that I can struggle when in the company of negative people for this reason!

Values are what we hold dear; they are important to us as standards for how we behave. Gaining some clarity on your own values is therefore important. One approach to doing this is to identify say the top five or six most important to you, with a bit of definition of what you mean by each. So, for example, what you mean by *fairness* might differ from what I would mean by it. That means defining your values is important.

With all this in mind, it is time to get a handle on your own values.

Exercise: Finding Your Values

Outlined in Table 7.1 is a list of 90 words that might represent values that are important to you. For many people, it is helpful to view a list of values words, like this one, to spark thinking about what their important values are. I have used this list many times during my professional career, particularly with business clients who are thinking about their future career direction. They provide particularly good evidence for the types of business culture an individual might work well in, for example a democratic culture as opposed to an autocratic one.

Table 7.1 List of values words

Acceptance	Expertise	Quietness
Achievement	Flexibility	Reasonableness
Advancement	Freedom	Recognition
Adventure	Friendship	Refinement
Affection	Growth	Relationships
Ambition	Harmony	Reliability
Authority	Health	Respect
Awareness	Helpfulness	Responsibility
Balance	Honesty	Responsiveness
Carefulness	Honor	Security
Challenge	Independence	Self-sufficiency
Clarity	Integrity	Sensitivity
Community	Involvement	Serenity
Competence	Justice	Simplicity
Competition	Learning	Solitude
Connection	Love	Sophistication
Consistency	Loyalty	Stability
Cooperation	Meaning	Status
Creativity	Modesty	Strength
Decisiveness	Naturalness	Supportiveness
Democracy	Nobility	Sympathy
Determination	Open-minded	Temperance
Development	Openness	Tolerance
Discretion	Order	Tranquility
Effectiveness	Participation	Truth
Efficiency	Patience	Understanding
Ethics	Pleasure	Uniformity
Empathy	Powerfulness	Variety
Excellence	Productivity	Wellness
Excitement	Purity	Wisdom

Remember, values are your moral compass or rules for how you want to do your work and live your life. You may well judge people, and entire organizations, by how they measure up to your values. So, for example, if you place a high value on *participation,* you might struggle to deal with someone who is dictatorial in nature.

The first step is to go through each of the 90 values, giving each one a mark out of five, where:

5 = critically important
4 = Significantly important
3 = of some importance
2 = little importance
1 = unimportant

The second step is to take only those values that you marked as a 5 and rank them in order of importance to you, starting with the most important. If you could only have one of your top values satisfied, which one would it be? Then if you could have a second value satisfied, which one would you then take? A third? Work through your list until you have five or six values that you see as most important to you.

If you are a harsh marker, you may not have many 5 scores. In this case, look through your 4 scores in the same way.

It's worth remembering that you should go for those values that are important to you, not the ones you think you ought to have. There are no right or wrong answers when it comes to what your most important values are.

The final step in this exercise is to define what you mean by each value, when you use the word. This may sound like a step too far, especially if you don't do detail. Let me explain why this step matters, with an example. For this, we'll use Tom and Anne. They both came up with *Democracy* as a key value for themselves.

Tom defined *democracy* as "being included in all key decisions that affect me."

Meanwhile, Anne's definition for it was "the chance to participate in what's going on and debate issues in depth."

One definition emphasizes self-empowerment and decisions, while the other emphasizes participation and debate. Both are about *democracy*, but they are different.

So what do you mean when you refer to your values? Take some time out now and define what you mean by each one.

Values and Power

Just how are your values relevant to power? In some ways, their effect is like your purpose. The key difference is that purpose is where you want to go, while values are how you get there, or what standards you want to hold to during your journey. If your values are being violated, you will know about it usually by how you feel. Can you think of a time, for example when you were asked to do something you didn't want to do?

Here's an example where someone faced just this situation in their workplace:

> OK, one example is when I was asked to make people redundant a few years back. I was new to the job and wanted to be a good manager for the team. But before I could get my feet under the table, I was given a list of people to get rid of, and I had to get rid of them. I didn't like that. I felt put upon, dumped on, angry, annoyed, because I was asked to carry out a decision that I had no say in, and which I wasn't sure had been taken on fair grounds.

Clearly from this example, your feelings and emotions will tell you where your values are being violated. Once you realize this, you can choose what to do about it.

Putting Purpose and Values Together

Understanding your purpose and values allows you to choose where to focus your power. For example, let's say that your colleague decides for some reason not to consult you about something. What should you do about it? The answer is that it depends whether the issue is important to you. It is your purpose and values that will let you know the extent to which it is important.

If it's unimportant, you might let it go or make a mild comment about being left out of the loop. But if it is important to you, a more powerful response might be needed. The response options you have will be dealt with in subsequent steps to ethical power. The key point here is you can make an informed decision about what to do. If you're unclear about your purpose and values, then you will be making subconscious decisions about how you react to situations and people. What's more, your reactions are likely to be more instinctive; whatever it is that you normally do. For most people, *normal* means the choice between fight, flight, and freeze, which we talked about earlier in the book. Another way to say this is we default to our childhood response to a perceived threat, without any real evaluation of the issue.

To use the compass and horizon analogy, let's say we're sailing to a point on the horizon. Then a big wave crashes over our side and changes the direction of the boat. What do we do? If we know where we want to go, and we have a good compass, we can make a judgment call on whether to go with the flow or reposition our boat. But without a point on the horizon to aim for and a compass, we are simply left with the choice of fighting the wave and looking tough (i.e., steering into it) or letting the wave win and going with the flow. We do whatever comes spontaneously to our nature, and whether we're still heading in the right direction for us is anyone's guess.

In short, our purpose gives us a sense of direction; our values give us an early warning system. Without them, we have no direction, no anchor. Without them, we place ourselves out of power. All we can do then is to react to how others use their power. We will always be choosing whether to comply with or to fight those who are defining the agenda. We will never get to define our own agenda. It's a bit like being in opposition in our lives and never governing it. We've all had work colleagues who are basically against everything or who just go along with everything. They never actually state clearly what they are for. Often it is as simple as not being clear about their own purpose and values. I really can't state the importance of this often enough.

"Now" and "Big"

Two other words are important, and those words are *now* and *big*. Do it now, and do it big, not small and later. Your purpose and values are too important for *small and later* to be the mantra. Indeed, your life and your work are too important! Too many people out there procrastinate over why now is not the right time or start with small steps and forget to take any big ones. Life is far too short for that.

Now you might say that this goes against conventional wisdom when it comes to making changes in your life. Conventional wisdom says that you should take small steps first. So, let me get on my soapbox; then you can make a choice. It's your life after all. I remember seeing a study a few years back. In this study, hundreds of people were interviewed, and these people were near the end of their lives. They were either very old, or they were dying and knew they were. The aim was to find out what lessons they would like to pass on to younger generations. There were three main lessons that were passed on. First, don't worry about the small stuff. Don't waste your life fretting over small details, or day-to-day stuff, as it usually ends up looking after itself. Second, take every opportunity to tell those close to you how you feel about them, especially those you love. Third, it's not the things you do that you regret, it's what you didn't do.[1]

What this means is thinking big, doing big, living a big life, and not putting off what really matters. No one ever achieved anything by aiming low. Unless you are a limbo dancer you should raise the bar.

It was Anthony Robbins in his seminal book *Awaken the Giant within*, who pointed out the importance of creating your own future vision, your "magnificent obsession."[2] Setting out your own compelling future would help to generate both energy and momentum. Of course, we already know that energy and momentum are closely related to personal power.

You are the only person around with your specific purpose and personal values, experiences and background. There isn't another one of you. You are a unique individual. It's up to you to maximize your power base and make your truly unique contribution to the world. That is, if you want to. Those words *big* and *now* will help to make it happen. But beware! Most people say they want to make it happen when asked; but when it comes to reality they choose to lose their power, or even in some cases abuse it. Think back to the first lesson that the elderly wanted to tell us, about not worrying about the small stuff. Sometimes small stuff is just day-to-day activities: worrying about laundry, doing filing, paying bills, and the like. But sometimes a bigger drain on time is the use of diversions, and we all use these.

For example, many people use humor as a diversion. Now, don't get me wrong; there is a role in life for wit, repartee, and maybe even sarcasm. But it can be overused or used to cover up what's really going on. As we saw in Chapter 4, humor can be a sign that we've lost our power. But some of us use it to willfully lose our power without anyone else inviting us to do so. Some people put themselves down through their use of humor, undermining their own power. Now a little self-deprecation isn't necessarily bad. But when it becomes a regular habit, then take a long hard look at what it's doing to your power. Putting yourself down all the time is not a good move.

Humor is only one diversion. There are others, some of which we've already encountered in this book. Some people spend a lot of time focusing on the trivial, the very small stuff. Some people choose to gossip over the lives of other people rather than look at their own. Some adopt an extreme interest in something or other, like seeing every work of William Shakespeare in theater, watching every reality TV program going, or climbing every mountain above 1,000 meters. I could go on.

In putting purpose and values together, purpose is the *where* and values are the *how*. They answer the questions "where do I want to go" and "how do I want to get there." It's worth noting that purpose has nothing to do with the *what*. Purpose is focused on direction, whereas the question *what* is focused on activity. As we often see in the Western world, activity does not equal achievement or progress. Being active and busy and getting somewhere are not the same thing. The difference between *where* and *what* is critical if we are to really get somewhere.

Exercise: Putting Purpose and Values Together

For this exercise, I'd like you to take the work you've already done on your purpose and values and consider the following questions designed to help you to put your purpose and values together.

1. Look again at your own purpose and values; what are your initial thoughts and conclusions?
2. Now return to the empowerment audit you carried out in Chapter 6. What impact have your life purpose and personal values had on the scores you gave yourself in that audit?
3. Where are the important areas in your career and life that you now need to focus on and sort out?

When the Situation Matters

Where someone cuts across our power and it does matter to us, I've always found the following model useful in making decisions on what to do next. The model focuses on comparing our concern for the substance of an issue (i.e., How important it is for me?) with our concern for maintaining the quality of the relationship with the other person. The model in Figure 7.1 was developed by two behavioral scientists, Ralph Kilmann and Kenneth Thomas[3], and is called the conflict mode instrument.

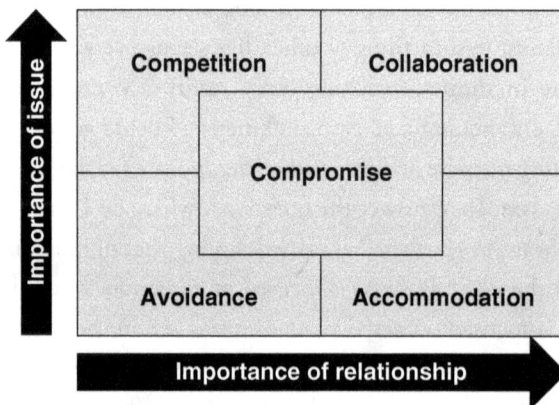

Figure 7.1 *The Thomas Kilmann model*

Based on this model, you have five influencing approaches you can use, depending on the situation.

Competition

In this case, the issue is more important to you than the relationship is, at least in the short term. Where this is true, competing may be the appropriate style to adopt, and in extreme circumstances it may mean trying to win at all costs. You choose to pursue your own issue at the other person's expense if necessary. It may entail standing up for your own rights, or defending your own position, which is important to you. You might also believe that your view is correct. The risk is if the other person feels the same way, the result will be conflict.

Collaboration

Here, both the issue and the relationship are important to you, making collaboration a desirable option. When you collaborate, you sit down with the other person and try to work out a win–win solution that gives both parties what they are looking for. You work with the other person to find a solution that fully satisfies you both. You may need acceptance and commitment from the other person if you are to get what you need out of the situation. This option is great for building long-term relationships without sacrificing what's important to you. However, collaboration is time-consuming; relying on it all the time is not likely to be very productive.

Compromise

Here, both the issue and the relationship have some importance to you. However, they aren't as important as for the collaboration option. This may mean that the best solution is simply to split the difference, with both parties getting something out of the agreement and giving something up. The solution ends up being an acceptable one, not an ideal one. Compromise can be a faster option than collaboration when there's time pressure, and it accepts that there may be situations where one person winning will mean the other person losing.

Accommodation

With accommodation, your need to sustain the relationship is greater than the importance of the issue at stake. In this case, you accommodate the other person's needs, while perhaps trying to get out of the situation what you can. You give up your concerns for the issue to satisfy the concerns of the other person. You may decide to accommodate for reasons of goodwill or to preserve harmony. You sacrifice something that isn't overimportant to you in favor of someone else, for whom the issue is more important.

Avoidance

As the term suggests, both the relationship and the issue are unimportant to you. So, you may simply decide to avoid the issue and the person concerned. Metaphorically speaking, you put your head in the sand. You do not try to pursue either your own needs or the needs of the other person. You may choose to diplomatically sidestep something if it is trivial in your opinion.

৯৹

All these approaches can be valid where used appropriately. However, the risk is that these different approaches may be used in the wrong situations. For example, the person who competes because they see every situation as a win–lose one, and they always want to win even where the issue is trivial. More common is the person who gives up too easily on what they want and avoids or accommodates when they should be considering more active options.

The value of the fifth step to ethical power is that it highlights how important the issue (and perhaps the relationship) is to you. If it is important, then the options for you are to collaborate, compete, or compromise. The other options are running away from what matters to you. The next few chapters consider how to use this model, to deal with important issues, and to preserve important relationships.

Summary

In this chapter, we have explored the fifth principle of ethical power, which is to get clear on what matters to you. You do this by connecting with your own purpose and personal values. Getting clear on these will give you a greater sense of direction in your life and tell you where you need to exert your personal power. You have spent some time working on identifying your own purpose and personal values.

Let's summarize the importance of your own personal clarity. If we make sure we're clear about our purpose and values, we can generate real momentum around our own power. It will be clearer when our power is under threat and we are being blocked from doing what matters to us. It's important to pursue our direction now, not later, and to aim high rather than settle for mediocrity. Finally, like the river, if we resist the temptation to divert our flow down other small, meaningless channels, we will have more energy for our main flow toward our purpose.

This clarity will raise the level of your river to increase its power; in other words, to raise your overall energy levels. But it still leaves a question around what we do about the rocks in the river, referred to in the last chapter. A strong, high river has a greater chance of getting around or over the rocks, but the rocks are still there. The next lesson begins to look at what to do when you encounter those rocks, and particularly when they are thrown by other people.

PART 3

Applying Your Power Ethically

CHAPTER 8

Undressing Power

The key to successful leadership today is influence, not authority.
—Ken Blanchard

The sixth step to ethical power—Undress power

The sixth step to ethical power is to undress power. Where you notice other people undermining your power, it's important that you let them know the impact they're having on you, to bring it into the open. Doing this ethically and respectfully will allow other people to change their behavior toward you, without undermining their own power.

Introduction

So far, we have looked at how you can assess your own state of power in different situations and over time. This is effective in diagnosing your levels of empowerment. Then in the last chapter, we examined the importance of working out what really matters to you, setting some sort of direction for your career and in your life.

The sixth step to ethical power puts these two parts together, to allow you to act when someone challenges your power, and it matters to you. Step 6 is the one you take when you need to assert your rights because in some way they are under threat.

More specifically, there are three elements present when you need to invoke Step 6 to ethical power. These elements are listed below:

1. Someone, somewhere has done something to you or alternatively not done something. Either way, their action has had an impact on you, reducing or otherwise undermining your power.

2. You notice your own emotional reaction to what's happened. For example, let's say a work colleague has put you down in public, and belittled your project. Your emotional reaction could be one of many—anger, annoyance, irritation, you might feel small, or put down. Whatever it is, you've connected with a feeling that's true for you.

3. You decide that this is a battle worth fighting by referring to the fifth step to ethical power outlined in the last chapter. You realize that the impact on your power by the action taken really does matter to you. Consequently, you will feel like you ought to say something to them about what they've done or not done.

We will shortly look at a technique you can use to expose this threat to your power and to ask for it to stop in future. However, first, let's return to a theme from Chapter 4 of this book; the notion that power is often undermined subtly in the modern workplace, not to mention society. This increasing subtlety makes it even more important to be vigilant about what's happening to our power, as it can be taken away by stealth if we're not careful.

The Modern Cloaks for Power

Let's explore the subtlety of the power theme a little more. The challenge in modern life is that we can easily miss the ways that we become disempowered if we're not careful. I want to highlight three ways this can happen; I call them the modern cloaks for power. In some ways, they have always existed, but in modern life the way they are used is subtler than say 50 to 100 years ago. In some parts of the world, their use is more blatant, but in the West this blatancy is not openly encouraged.

These cloaks are expertise, learning, and faith. Of course, many people would say that these are good things. To develop expertise, to want to learn, and to have faith in something are good things are they not? That is precisely the reason why they make such effective cloaks for undermining power. Disempowering others is less obviously an abuse if it is covered up by something sugary that looks nice, or virtuous, or desirable.

The other point to be made about expertise, learning, and faith is that they are all ways to control the behavior of other people and therefore of us. So, we need to be vigilant where this is happening. The key tool of vigilance, of course, is how we feel about what is going on. Let's look at each of the three cloaks a bit more.

The Role of "Expertise"

Expert power is a risk in modern life and an even bigger risk in modern business. Let's illustrate this fact with one simple example. Consider the global economic recession from 2008, and what has happened since. Most people now agree that the actions of the banks, property investors, and the wider financial services industry carry a significant degree of responsibility for the chain of events that led to the recession.

Consider the role of hedge funds and the part they played in the economic and financial collapse that led to banks throughout the world either collapsing or being bailed out by governments. In recent years, it has been openly admitted that many people in the industry who worked with hedge funds actually had no idea how they operated. Even the *experts* weren't all that expert.

There are experts everywhere. For example, look at human rights legislation, employment law, complex tax, and financial laws, baffling ranges of choice in insurance and pensions, changes in information technology that take longer and longer to explain. The role of expert is all pervasive in modern life, and the risk we run as individuals is that it's impossible to know everything about everything. That can put us under the power of the expert, and they might not use their expertise in our interests. It's true to say that never have we had so much information and so little knowledge. Clearly, expertise is important sometimes, and experts can be useful. But we need to be vigilant for those instances where experts are using us.

The Role of Learning

One obvious example of an attempt to justify power over another person would be *I know more than you do about this.* It might be because I'm more qualified than you, or because you are a trainee or new to the job. Sometimes my taking power might be justified, but not always. I might abuse my power as teacher and use your alleged lack of knowledge to justify my superiority.

In the old days, an employee with 10 years' experience would hold more power than someone with only 8 years of experience, simply because they've been around for longer. So the assumption is that they know more.

This approach is not very clever. Einstein was a school pupil once, and Shakespeare would have had to learn how to speak English properly in the first place. In the case of Einstein, he was famously dismissed by his Munich schoolmaster, who reported that he didn't think Einstein would amount to very much. To use a pun, he went on to do relatively well!

The thing about learning is that it can be a means of control. To get this qualification, or this qualified job, you'd better think this way. Otherwise, you won't get there. That approach discourages independent, critical thinking by controlling what people think; in other words, by curbing their power. Then of course, there are professional institutes and bodies that largely operate the same way. Of course, it doesn't happen in a *comply or die* sort of way. It's subtler than that.

The Role of Faith

Historically, religion has proven even more powerful to keep people under control. It was Karl Marx who described religion as "the opium of the people."[1] By this, I think he meant that the promise of a better life after death led to people often accepting miserable life conditions in this life. The role of religious belief and authority is, in many cases, one of the key disempowering factors in people's lives. The history of world religion is one big power struggle that continues even to this day.

The key religions adopt the same basic principles. There is a holy text, which is interpreted by those in authority in that religion, who then tell the rest of us what it all means, and therefore what to believe. Our role in this is to suspend our own judgment and to have faith. The deal we are given is that if we do good deeds in this life (however they are defined), then we can hope to be rewarded in the afterlife.

The trouble with this approach is that, depending who we are talking about, good deeds can include giving up some or all of your money to the church, suicide bombing a market, or fighting a war. If the God as portrayed by religion had been human, I have little doubt that he would be referred to a psychiatrist.

Of course, religious and spiritual belief can be a force for good. You need look no further than to the likes of Gandhi, Mother Teresa, Martin Luther King, or the Dalai Lama for evidence of that. However, it is often used as a cloak to remove people's power, and it is this we should beware of.

Of course, messianic forces have frequently appeared at the top of businesses too; from Steve Jobs at Apple to Jean-Marie Messier at Vivendi and Fred Goodwin at the Royal Bank of Scotland. Forceful leaders who are able to be charismatic can convert followers into a near-religious fervor or at least to suspend their own judgment—and that entails suspending our own power.

Undressing the Power Cloaks

The necessary precondition to the sixth step to ethical power is that we notice our loss of power in the first place. We talked in Chapter 4 about the giveaway signs that we're becoming disempowered, and the single most important sign is how you feel at the time.

As mentioned at the beginning of this chapter, you then need to decide whether this is a battle worth fighting. You do that by referring to your own purpose, and your personal values, and deciding whether this is an important enough issue to tackle. In the language of the Thomas Kilmann conflict model discussed in the last chapter, you are effectively deciding that the issue needs to be competed over, collaborated on, or compromised to a degree.

You need to make sure you are clear about whether the issue is important enough or whether you prefer to live with it, because if you decide to live with it you must live with it. It's not good enough to complain about it afterward. In other words, make your decision and live with the consequences.

If you decide it is a battle worth fighting, the next step is to *name* what's happening. *Naming* it is another way of saying *bring it out into the open* so that you and the other person or people are aware both of what is going on, and the fact that you know it. Bear in mind at this stage that the other person may not actually be aware of their impact on you. Simply bringing it to their attention will help to resolve the issue. However, if they were aware of what they were doing, they will now know that you know what they're doing. It is, of course, important to do this in a way that makes it easier for the other person to accept.

Case Study: The Critical Boss

Emily is in her mid-40s and works in a professional office-based job as a team leader. She dreads going into her boss's office, as he only ever calls Emily in when it's bad news. His manner is brusque and condescending. What's worse, he isn't averse to criticizing Emily in public, in front of the rest of her colleagues. The fact that he does this with everybody doesn't help, as it leaves Emily feeling upset. Emily decides to do something about this.

What is the key point Emily wants to get across?

"The main thing, I suppose, is that he seems to end up criticizing me in front of other people, leaving me humiliated and embarrassed. It means I have less credibility with the other people I work with. If he has something to say, I'd prefer to hear it from him one to one. I'd also feel more able to have a conversation with my manager if I have a different point of view about what happened."

Given Emily's view, one option is to say something to her boss, along the following lines:

When you are critical of what I do in public, it undermines my position and makes it more difficult for me to do my job effectively. I'd prefer it if you could share any comments you have about what I'm doing with me beforehand.

Emily could go on to suggest one-to-one meetings. But what she is doing here is making it clear in a reasonable way that her boss is undermining her power.

It is possible that challenging people in this way might generate some resistance from them; in other words, they might argue back at the time. Alternatively, they might agree with you, but not go on to change their behavior. It is therefore important that you stick to your position and avoid the temptation to back down. In the next chapter, we will look at a couple of approaches that will help with this.

When challenging other people's impact on your own power, you are deciding to *undress* their impact on your power by bringing it into the open. But how should you undress power? There are three basic parts to how you do this. First, tell the person what they've done or not done. Second, tell them about the impact of their action and how you feel about it. Third, tell them how you'd like them to behave in future.

Applying these rules to the example above, Emily might say something like this.

- When you put me down in that last meeting
- I felt annoyed
- In future, I want you to stop doing this in public. If you have an issue with my work, please talk to me one to one.

The great thing with this approach is that it's to the point. The other person can have no doubt about what they did, its impact on you, and what you want to happen in future. Furthermore, by talking about your feeling in Step 2, you effectively remove any scope for an argument. The other person can't argue with how you feel, after all. Even if they try to justify their actions, they can't remove the fact that you felt bad.

That illustrates the power in sometimes talking about feelings. They are hard to argue against. The irony is that people sometimes avoid talking about feelings because they think it makes them look weak!

It is important to do it in an ethical, respectful way, so that the other person doesn't feel that you've undermined their power or crossed a line with them. It is equally important to make your statements honestly. Don't say you feel devastated if your feeling is nothing like as powerful as this. Save strong words for when you really do feel that strongly. Equally, don't downgrade your own feeling or dress up your comment in a cloak of diplomacy. If someone has undermined your power, they need to be told that. Keep your comment brief; using lots of words simply dilutes the message.

Exercise: Undressing Power

Think of a situation from the past where someone else's behavior impacted on your power. Work through the questions, coming to a diagnosis on how you tackled the situation you've come up with.

1. Describe the situation and the other person's actions.
2. How did this action impact on your power? Why did it matter to you?
3. How did you handle the situation at the time? Did it work?
4. In hindsight, how would you have changed your handling of this situation?
5. If you had used the sixth step to ethical power, write down exactly what you would have said to the person in question, using the following formula—When you..........I felt............In future, I'd like you to............

℘

Once you have made the undressing statement in real life, the conversation could go one of several ways. The other person may be shocked at the impact they've had, as they may have been unaware that their behavior even affected you. In this case, you will probably get an apology, and the issue will be sorted out. Many people are oblivious to the impact of their words and actions, and so perhaps are we at times. Having that impact pointed out to us in a respectful way can be helpful.

In a few cases, the other person may not care or think you're overreacting to what they've done. In these cases, you may need to escalate your assertion (which is dealt with in the next chapter) or continue the conversation with the person about what happened. But at least you've brought the issue to their attention by taking Step 6 and saying something.

Helping Others to Change

There is a possibility that what you say might generate some resistance from the other person. They may attempt to justify their behavior, and in some cases, might even deny it. In these cases, one useful approach is to consider what it is that helps people to change what they do.

It's a very simple tool and great for analyzing what might need to change if you are to avoid becoming disempowered in different situations. It's called the change equation,[2] and it originated from work undertaken by Richard Beckhard and Reuben T. Harris in 1987.

The Change Equation

The equation is an approach to analyzing why change either does or does not occur. It is particularly useful in business change situations, and how to maximize the chances of successful change. It can also be applied to people as well as situations, allowing us to identify why people change what they do sometimes, and at other times why they don't. The starting point is that there are three things that need to be in place before people will consider changing some aspect of what they do.

First, they need to have a clear *vision* of what it is they want to change. In other words, if they make the change, they can see a vision for how things will be in the future. It is important, of course, that what they see is an attractive future!

Second, they need to be *discontented* in some way with where they are today. The greater the discontent, the more likely it is that people will want to make a change. When they get sufficiently discontented, they will be desperate to make any change!

Third, they need to know from a practical point of view, what are the *first steps* they need to take to make the change happen. They may not know the whole journey, but they need some idea of the first two or three actions to take (or what to stop doing).

The stronger each of these elements is, the better the chances of getting change to happen. However, there is another element in play: What are the *costs* of changing? Making a change usually costs us something; that's why it's often difficult to change in the first place. The cost could be financial, of course. It could be the cost of losing something that we enjoy, such as moving away from a team we've enjoyed working with. It could be the psychological cost of change, for example of changing a habit we have. Of course, taking all these different costs into account, the higher the costs of change, the less likely it is that we will change.

We can represent the change equation in the following way:

Where $V \times D \times F > C$, change will happen.

Where $V \times D \times F < C$, change will not happen

Where V = vision for how things could be in the future, D = discontent with the current situation, F = knowledge of first steps to be taken to make change happen, and C = costs of change (personal, financial, psychological).

When it comes to power, we may want to encourage someone else to change their behavior toward us. This equation can be very useful in working out what to do. Here are a few strategies you could adopt to try to change the balance of someone else's change equation.

You could raise the value of D, their level of discontent with the current situation, by:

- Pointing out the effect of their current behavior on you. Most people don't want to think they are adversely affecting others, so highlighting this alone might stop the behavior.
- If the other person is disempowering you in their attempt to achieve something, highlight the adverse consequences to their objective if they continue the current pattern of behavior.
- If all this fails, then simply giving them grief because they are continuing to undermine your power might work. So, continuing to raise the problem with them can be a good strategy. Have you ever noticed how some people who are a continually nagging pain in the backside often end up getting their way? This is how they do that.

You could raise the value of V, their vision of a potential future, by:

- Talking about how attractive the future could be for them if their current behavior was changed.

You could raise the value of F, their understanding of the first steps to take to begin changing, by:

- Making clear what the specific changes are that you are looking for.
- Saying how you are prepared to change in return.

You could lower the value of C, their perceived cost of change, by:

- Offering support to the other person to help them change what you need them to change.
- Giving them something else as an incentive, maybe on a "you scratch my back and I'll scratch your back" basis.

The change equation is a very simple, yet effective, approach to encouraging people to change their behavior. When someone's behavior or actions are getting in your way, it is worth considering what influence you might have over their equation.

Making Resistance Futile

In Chapter 5, we talked about the ways we use to sometimes resist change, and that this approach can have the effect of disempowering us. To remind ourselves, there are many ways in which we can resist change. Here are just three of the resistance strategies we talked about:

- *Moralizing*—Where we moralize about the situation or find someone else to blame. "Of course, I understand what needs to be done, but they don't!" Or "If it wasn't for that lot, we wouldn't need to do this."
- *No time*—"I don't have time to do this" or "now is not the right time."
- *Real world*—"Now this might be a great idea in principle, but in the real world, it'll never work!"

Of course, when we looked at resistance earlier, we were looking at our own resistance. However, of equal importance are those situations where we notice other people resisting the things we try to do. We might notice resistance when we are undressing their power over us and starting to make clear what we'd like to happen.

So, what do we do when we notice someone else resisting our approach? One option is to *name* the resistance we face. In other words, we undress it to bring the resistance out into the open. Peter Block[3] came up with a useful approach to use when other people resist, which can be applied to situations where they are resisting change in favor of continuing to disempower you. His formula was that you do the following:

1. On the first couple of occasions, you allow the other person's resistance to be expressed in good faith. In other words, don't initially assume it is resistance. So, to take one of the above resistance approaches, you might allow the other person to do a bit of moralizing without assuming that it's an expression of resistance. They may just want to get some frustration off their chest, for example.

2. If it happens a third time, it's time to name the resistance, without blaming the other person. Give the feedback using words like "I'm sensing" or "I'm noticing that . . ." In the moralizing example above, you might say something like "I'm noticing that whenever I talk about this issue, you talk about what other people should be doing."

3. Having undressed the resistance, you either say nothing or ask an open-ended question like "what's going on for you?" After the question, you say nothing. It's vital if this approach is to work that the other person speaks next.

4. Actively listen to whatever the other person says at this stage, whether it is rationally thought through or more emotional. At this point, there is an opportunity for a more productive conversation, focusing on the real issues rather than resorting to power cloaks and resistance approaches.

5. If you need to move the conversation further, try saying simply how this is making you feel. This means going back to the second step to ethical power in Chapter 4, and not only recognizing how you feel at the time but being willing to express it to the other person. Make sure you express it in a way that avoids placing blame on the other person. There is a world of difference between the following two ways of making the same point:

   "I feel frustrated at this situation at the moment."

   "Your behavior is making me feel frustrated."

The second approach is much more likely to provoke an argument. Even worse than that would be *you frustrate me*. That comment will guarantee fireworks!

It may also be that you want to reinforce what it is that you wish to happen or not happen. At this stage, we move from undressing power to redressing it, which we cover in the next chapter. But first, let's consider an example.

An Example of Undressing Resistance

Samantha is an office manager, who has been asked by her manager to implement a new piece of software throughout her office. It means asking her team to change the way they work, as well as having to complete a training package before using it. The new software cannot be fully utilized, however, until everyone in her team is using it. Only then can the old system be switched off, allowing her administrative staff to save a lot of time—and improve customer service into the bargain.

Samantha has asked to see one of her team members Steve. Steve has been diligent in *not* taking up the new software. Nor has he completed the training package, which would be one of the first steps to take. The conversation goes as follows:

Sam: I wanted to find out how you're getting on with the new software, Steve.

Steve: Well, uhm, it looks quite good, I must admit. Things are busy out there just now, lots of customer issues to deal with. I haven't been able to get time to look at it.

Sam: If you remember, at the last team meeting, I agreed to let everyone have 3 hours this month to do the training.

Steve: Yes, you did. But I know that Anthea and Jim did the course partly in their own time. You know I have a long journey to work, so that is less of an option for me.

Sam: When do you think you might be able to do this? We don't get the benefits from this new software until everybody is using it.

Steve: It's hard. I know I'm one of the last, but I have loads to get on with. I'll try to do it in the next couple of weeks, but time is short just now.

(Continued)

> Sam: I'm noticing Steve that when we talk about the software change, you say you don't have time to do this. What's going on for you here?
>
> Silence—5 seconds
>
> Steve: What do you mean?
>
> Sam: I notice that time seems to be a big issue for you on this.
>
> Steve: To be honest, I have lots going on at home right now. Also, I did look at the software online, and it looks rather complicated to me. You know that IT isn't my strongest point. I like dealing with customers and solving their problems, and this software might take all my time and stop me from doing what I enjoy. Besides, I don't feel very confident looking at it.
>
> Sam: So, you're concerned that your job might be less enjoyable in future. In addition, you seem worried about whether you'll be able to cope with the new software system?
>
> Steve: Yes, and things are a bit hectic at home, which isn't helping.

At this stage, Samantha has surfaced some of the reasons why Steve is resisting the change. Fear of IT, concern that it might make his job less interesting, and possibly something going on at home are the reasons Steve is resisting. Time has little to do with it. With this information, Samantha can have a real conversation to try to help Steve. She might be able to give him more time to train. She might be able to reassure him over the job, and that he will spend at least as much time as before doing the things he enjoys. But at least it will be a real conversation about what's really going on, rather than a resistance tug-of-war.

That is the real value of undressing the resistance.

Summary

In this chapter, we have explored the sixth principle of ethical power, which is to undress power on those occasions when other people are disempowering you, to bring this fact out into the open. You have spent some time working on your own technique to use in situations that might merit this approach.

We talked about the three cloaks for power: expertise, learning, and faith. On the surface, they are often seen as desirable things to have in our lives. However, they can all be misused in a way that takes our power away if we're not careful. Where we notice our power being taken away, a good technique to use is to name it. In other words, I can undress what's going on, to point out that I've noticed this. We also looked at the change equation, which can be used to encourage other people to change their behavior toward us.

Let me summarize a bigger picture. We looked a little while ago at getting clear about what matters to you in your professional and personal life: your purpose, personal values, aiming big, and all that stuff. We've just looked at what you could do when you notice someone else tampering or interfering with your own power, particularly where you decide that it is preventing you from achieving the things that really matter to you.

However, Step 6 is essentially a reactive approach to asserting your power. It is what you do when someone has crossed a line with you. You are responding to other people who are interfering with you in some way. However, if we want to achieve the things we set out to do, then we need to be more proactive than this sometimes. In Step 7, we look at how asserting your power looks when it is done proactively. It's time to make it clear to others what it is you're trying to achieve, and where it is you're trying to go.

CHAPTER 9

Redressing Power

I never give them hell. I just tell the truth and they think it's hell.
—Harry S. Truman

The seventh step to ethical power—Redress power

The seventh step to ethical power is to use assertive behaviors to build your power base up with others. Be proactive, make decisions, act on them, and take responsibility for them. Recognize that sometimes it may be better to seek forgiveness than to seek permission.

Introduction

In my conversations with business people, it's clear that most people want to have more control over their work, moving it in a direction they want to go in. The seventh step to ethical power is about saying what you want and where you want to head.

This is the step that most people have the greatest difficulty with in exercising ethical power. But it is a key to achieving the things we really want and to be the person we want to be.

It is ironic that so many people struggle with this step. Why? Because we are born with this talent. Yes, born with it! If you doubt this, just think back to your childhood, or look at children you know now. I have never met a 3-year-old who doesn't know how to be powerful. Kids scream the place down, and they know how to exercise their lungs;

it's only adults who mumble. Young children know how to assert them-selves in spades:

"I want a bar of chocolate!"
"I'm hungry!"
"I want you to let me out to play!"

Indeed, the first thing a baby does is announce its arrival into the world by screaming his or her head off. Yet we lose this volume as we grow up. We lose the ability to be powerful in many cases too. We become a toned-down version of our younger selves.

This step is about being assertive, about pushing your own agenda. Otherwise other people don't know what your agenda is. Other people cannot help or avoid hindering you if they don't know what you're trying to do. The key is for you to be up front with others about your intentions.

There are two main ways you can use to be up front. These are *being rational* and *being powerful.* Let's look at both options in a little more detail.

Being Rational

Here, you state your case in a rational way, giving reasons in support of what you're proposing. For example, imagine for a moment that I have been talking you through the contents of this book for the last couple of hours, and it's now getting late. I might decide to be rational and say to you:

"I think we should call it a night. My reasons are firstly, that we're both tired and need a rest. Secondly, it will benefit you more to practice what you've already learned rather than be swamped by further information."

Being rational is an effective way to exert your power when you have a good case for what you think should be done and reasons for it. Other key points about being rational include:

1. Not using too many reasons. Use two or three good, strong reasons and limit it to that. If you give more reasons than this, you expose your argument to more lines of possible attack from people who disagree with you.

2. Where you are able to, you should tailor your reasons to appeal to the interests of whoever you are talking to. This is like the idea of influencing the change equation in other people's heads that we spoke of in the last chapter.

3. Use *being rational* when you are open to rational counter arguments. While you have a view, you are open to debate and to possibly changing you view. If you're not open to counter arguments, don't use the being rational option. Use the second option we'll go on to look at in this chapter.

How to Be Rational

Definition: Making a proposal and backing it up with reasons.

When to do it: When you have a rational proposal or suggestion to make. Use being rational when you are open to influence on grounds of rational, logical argument.

The main parts of the *being rational* style:

- A proposal, suggestion, or recommendation.
- Use the word *I* to take responsibility for your proposal.
- Back up your proposal with the one or two best reasons.
- Don't ramble on or use too many reasons.

Words to use: I propose/suggest/recommend that . . .
My reasons for this are . . . firstly . . . secondly . . .

Tone of voice:

- Speak in a measured pace, don't talk too quickly.
- Calm, logical, with conviction but not over forceful.
- Rational, not emotional.

The Power of Being Rational

Being rational tends to be the language of business, and there are some good reasons why this is the case. For one thing, it is generally viewed as more appropriate to use rational argument rather than to over-rely on emotional points. There is also evidence that a reasoning, rational approach can impact significantly on the behavior of other people. For example, one research project highlighted the impact of the word *because*. In an experiment, a queue of people waiting to use an office photocopying machine were asked by a person joining at the end "May I go to the head of the line?" Even this request saw 63 percent of the people in the line allow this individual to queue jump ahead of them. However, when the person added the phrase "because I have copies to make" the number of people who agreed increased to more than 90 percent![1] Another study highlighted that the use of rational behavior was statistically linked to more positive outcomes in the workplace.[2]

Being Powerful

This is the second assertive technique. Here, you assert what you would like, want, or need to happen. Some examples would be:

> "I want to go back to my hotel after this meeting."
> "I would like you to give me only the key points on this issue in no more than 5 minutes."
> "I need another meeting with you to finish off what we're talking about within the next month."

You should use *being powerful* when you want something to happen, or someone else to do something for you, or to cease doing something. Essentially, you are willing someone to take, or stop taking, a course of action. Other key points to bear in mind about being powerful include:

- Keep to the point. Don't waffle or fluff up what you say with too many words.
- Don't give reasons, as this would imply you are open to debate if better reasons are found for another course of action. When being powerful, you are asserting your will. If you are open for debate, you should use *being rational* instead.

- Decide how strongly you want to assert your will and choose words accordingly. Words like *I'd like, I request, I want,* or *I demand* convey different strengths of will. Don't overplay or underplay your strength of feeling.

It's important that your requests or wants are legitimate; they should be things that you have a legitimate right to ask for. Use this approach when you have a legitimate need or want of another person, or if you want to do something that's within your power to do.

How to Be Powerful

Definition: Making it clear what you want, need, or expect from someone else.

When to do it: Where you have a legitimate need, expectation, or want of another person.

The main parts of the *being powerful* style:

- A short statement of the want/need/expectation, without reasons.
- The use of the word *I* to take responsibility for your own want, need, or expectation.
- Persist and repeat if necessary, if the message doesn't get through first time.

Words to use:

Depending on your strength of emotion:

Can you . . . I suggest that you . . . I'd like you to . . . I want you to . . . I demand that you . . .

or

Can I . . . I suggest that I . . . I'd like to . . . I want to . . . I demand to . . .

Tone of voice:

- Determined, firm, and forceful if necessary.
- Don't talk too quickly.

Exercise: "Being Powerful" or "Being Rational?"

I am going to ask you to take an issue that you think or feel strongly about and where you need to influence someone (either an individual or a group).

Ideally, pick an issue that is still live for you. But, if you can't come up with one, pick an issue from the recent past, perhaps one where in hindsight you didn't get the outcome you hoped for.

Now answer the following questions.

1. What was the issue? Describe this in some detail.
2. What did you think or feel about it? Did your view come from your heart/gut or from your head? Be honest with your answer here!
3. Who did the issue affect? Who would have been affected by your approach to it?

   Based on your answers thus far, is your view based on your gut or is it a more rational view? If it's the former, then being powerful is the approach to take. If it's the latter, then being rational would be a better option.
4. Which is the better fit for you on this issue, being powerful or being rational?
5. Now construct the key statement you will make, using the above table for either being rational or being powerful. The key statement is the *crunch point* of the conversation, where you make your proposal, request, want, or demand.

For example:

- I propose that we work on this problem together. My reasons are . . . (being rational).
- I want you to work with me on this problem (being powerful).

Finally, stand in front of a mirror and practice delivering this statement until you are satisfied that you look and sound credible saying it.

Childhood Lessons on Power

In blunt terms, we are encouraged to give up much of our power in childhood. We learn to dampen down our needs in exchange for a better tomorrow. Politeness and conditioning tone us down to the point that we lose much of our power. It becomes unacceptable to make demands or requests in anything approaching a direct manner.

The problem with this is that, if we lose our ability, we may never achieve our career and life goals. We may never become who we really want to be. We may never achieve whatever purpose we set out for our lives. In the end, the ability to assert ourselves and our wants and needs will make the difference, particularly when others are preventing us from getting to where we need to get to. There are times when we need to make decisions and act on them. When someone is in your way, deliberately or otherwise, you need to be able to say something and to take responsibility for your own power.

Power and Permission

Some people are prevented from using their own power by the sense that they need permission from others before they fully use it. After all, it was in childhood for most of us that we were denied permission to use our power at least some of the time. Parental injunctions that "I want doesn't get," and "it's politer to keep quiet" rub off on us over time, and those lessons about dampening down our own power come from all angles and sources during our upbringing and into adulthood.

Should we always need permission to use our power? I agree with the notion that sometimes it might be better to seek forgiveness afterward than to seek permission beforehand. In other words, do not be afraid of using your own power when you need to; other people will cope with it. It is, of course, important to use it ethically, and we will say more about this in subsequent chapters. If what you want to do has good intent, is in line with whom you are, and is not directly harming other people, then it is legitimate to be powerful and act.

The Rational Trap: Avoiding Being Powerful

What happens if we lose our ability to say *I want* in childhood? What happens in adulthood? Well typically, we resort to a rational approach through our use of being rational. We talk from the head rather than from our gut. We try to come up with rational reasons to support what it is that we want.

Well, isn't this OK, I hear you ask? We're all working adults now, and we've seen from research that being rational can have significant impact. That means being rational is the thing to do, isn't it? To a degree, yes, but only to a degree. There is clearly a role for rational, well-constructed arguments in the modern workplace and in life. However, there is a pitfall with relying on rational argument as the tactic of choice to get what you want. I will illustrate the pitfall with an example.

In the workplace, your manager invites you to a consultation meeting on a proposal to make some sort of change at work. He presents a reasoned proposal with arguments in support of it. However, you and others see gaps in his reasoning, and as you have been invited to contribute, you do so. Despite your contributions, it eventually becomes clear that the consultation is a sham. The manager has already made his mind up what he wants, and you realize this. How do you feel?

I have seen this type of situation in workplaces more often than I care to recall, and the staff reactions are usually along these lines:

- What a waste of time for us all!
- I wish he'd just been honest and said at the start that he'd already decided.
- Consult me if you want my opinion. If you've decided, just tell me.

Exactly! When you choose to use being rational as your means to influence people, others will examine your rationality, and if they see a flaw or drawback they will highlight it. Being rational is fine, if you are open to influence on whatever you're proposing on grounds of logical argument. You should be prepared to alter your view if someone else comes up with a better argument.

This is hard to do though if you already know what you want to happen. In this case, why not just be honest and tell them? The manager in this example is not being powerful. Instead of saying *I have decided to do this,* he hides behind rational argument to try to get what he wants. The result is that everyone ends up dancing around the chairs in debate until it becomes clear that the team is being manipulated. What's more, everyone will know this, and realize their time has been wasted.

Of course, the risk for the manager is even greater. If he is weak and tries to avoid being seen as a manipulator, he might not even get his way on a decision that was important to him. Just how powerful is that?

I imagine that most of you will readily see the difference between being rational and being powerful. But many among you will struggle to see where you would choose to use being powerful, unless perhaps you had your back to the wall. Some of you might even feel that if you did have your back to the wall, you wouldn't feel powerful enough to consider using it anyway! One obvious reason why this might be the case is the belief, imbued in many of us from childhood, that it's rude to say *I want.*

I'm not suggesting we should all go around saying *I want I want* all the time. The world would be an intolerable place if that's all we ever did. But losing the ability to be powerful is to throw the baby out with the bathwater. There are moments in our lives when it is OK to say it. In fact, I would argue that it's rude not to. After all, how polite is it to not let people know what you want, so they know where they stand? If we argue rationally for something rather than assert ourselves, we will often end up bogged down in a clash of wills that is dressed up as rational argument.

Don't try to rationally argue for something you strongly desire instead of being powerful unless you're prepared not to get it because there's a better argument than yours. It is deceptive to other people and defeating to you.

Being Proactive and Responsible

There's a lot more to redressing power than simply choosing whether to be rational or powerful. Really powerful people don't just do these two things well; they are also proactive in pursuit of their goals. They understand that positive thinking isn't enough on its own. Powerful performance is about making decisions and acting on them. There is no such thing as a perfect decision or a perfect time to do something. Getting powerful results means not being afraid to make decisions. A second-best decision made in time is often better than the best decision made too late. But a decision on its own achieves nothing, unless it's followed up by action in support of it.

Motivation and commitment are different things. Being motivated to do something is like saying I want to do this thing sometime. To be committed means moving mountains to get it done and making sure I act come what may. It's important to be committed, and not just motivated. Your challenge is to make the commitment to regain your power rather than just being motivated to do it. So, make your decisions and act, be committed to your cause. There is one more thing to bear in mind though; powerful people take responsibility, and are seen to take responsibility, for their decisions. They don't hide behind other people or circumstances. It is not without irony that a former American President, Harry Truman, famously had a sign on his desk, which said "the buck stops here."

The important thing if you are to get somewhere with your life is to select the path of power more often than not. You can afford the odd lapse, if it is the odd one.

So, Step 7 on the road to ethical power is about taking responsibility for your own power. It is about saying what you want from others. However, many people bottle it in these moments. Let's see another example of what happens when the bottle goes.

Another manager I once knew came to see me about a problem team member. I was a human resources consultant at the time, meaning it was my role to discuss staff problems with managers and to offer advice. One of the manager's staff had a lateness problem. She was frequently late for work. In addition, she was slipshod with her work and often made errors, which other team members noticed and corrected. This was generating resentment in the team.

My advice was to have a conversation with the person in question, highlight these two issues, see what her response was, and take it from there. A few days later, I spoke to the manager to see how he got on.

The long and short of it is that he bottled the conversation. He did meet the staff member, but he dressed his critical comments up and added in lots of positive points about her performance, so as not to undermine her confidence. The result? She left the meeting, thinking her performance was good! The manager wasn't powerful and didn't get his message through. He hoped instead that she would "get the drift." Alas, she did not!

Forgiveness and Power

The above example highlights another consequence of not being powerful. During our follow-up conversation, it became clear to me that the manager was frustrated by his inability to convey the message. He was also resentful of his team member. Lack of power and resentment go together. When we're powerful where we need to be, it is a lot easier to be charitable the rest of the time, once we've made our views and wants clear. This manager was not powerful, so it's no surprise that he didn't feel charitable toward her. She will have noticed this on some level. He was sullen, wasn't jokey, and didn't treat her as well as the rest of the team.

Choose Your Times

The key to being powerful, and expressing your wants and needs, is to do this sparingly. Use it where you have a genuinely legitimate request of another person. Your emotions and understanding of your own direction will tell you when your need is legitimate.

Using this tactic all the time is not going to be legitimate, of course. We all know people who say I want or I need all the time. When people continuously make demands, it is simply aggressive behavior. But there are moments of truth, where your need is legitimate. No one else has the right to prevent you from living your life, after all. This step is the key step to ethical power that will enable you to do that by proactively setting out your position, direction, and wants of others.

Many people fear making this stand, and that is an irrational fear. We fear that life may become intolerable if we stand up for our wants and needs. We fear that our job may end up on the line. It isn't easy to overcome that fear, but sometimes even a life of conflict will end up feeling better than one of disempowerment. If you don't believe this, consider the following conversation with a coaching client who was in the middle of just this sort of conflict, having decided to make some changes in her professional and personal life:

Client: "I feel much better in myself if that's what you mean. I feel more in control of my life. Yet, most of what I've described is conflict. Why do I feel better then?"

Coach: "Maybe because you're having a say in what happens. That's not how you felt before."

The client's reaction confirmed this diagnosis.

Summary

In this chapter, we have explored the seventh principle of ethical power, which is to use assertive behaviors to build your power base up with others. Be proactive, make decisions, act on them, and take responsibility for them. You've explored the differences between being rational and being powerful, where it is appropriate to use them, and how to use them when you need to. Finally, you've had the opportunity to think through how you might use these approaches.

In many ways, what we have tackled in this step to ethical power are those situations where we want to proactively manage our lives and achieve the things we want to. However, it's important to realize that we do not exercise our power in a vacuum. We live in a society with all its pressure and power, and these pressures impact on us. We work in organizations with their own pressures and power structures. In the next chapter, we turn our attention to this area, and how to remain powerful in the face of wider collective organizations of people.

CHAPTER 10

Staying Individual and Connected

Don't compromise yourself. You are all you've got.

—Janis Joplin

The eighth step to ethical power—Stay individual and connected

The eighth step to ethical power is to remain a powerful individual in the face of the pressures that exist in society, such as the pressure to conform. Being authentic and courageous is key, as well as balancing your own unique individuality with the wider collective needs that exist. Truly powerful, influential people don't just conform to the majority.

Introduction

This is the step that deals explicitly with how we as unique individuals with our talents, approaches, and values deal with collective organizations and groups, including the workplace.

One of the challenges with exercising personal power is that we're not exercising it in a vacuum. I'm referring here to the power structures in society: political, education, businesses and work organizations, the media, religion, and many others. Collective groups and the way they behave hugely affect the context within which we operate as individuals. In addition, the strength of our closest relationships can constrain our attempts to empower ourselves. Consider what one business client suggested to me during a coaching session:

> To be honest, I'm a bit fearful of what will happen when I do start changing things. I've read in the past that often it's the people closest to you who most resist you changing things, as potentially they are the ones that have most to lose.

You are surrounded by people who are used to you being just the way you are, be it at home or at work. When you start to change, it affects them, whether they like it or not. This step to ethical power is about not succumbing to the resistance of those around you. But nor is it about trampling on other people. We need to not succumb ethically.

So, what is this eighth step? It is to recognize the power of the collective relationships and organizations that we are part of, by choice or otherwise. You need to recognize their power but be true to yourself. Making your stand when it matters to you is important. Simply conforming to authority is not the key to happiness or to success. Conformity is the key to subordination, and even if you succeed by this route in some way, it will not feel like success to you.

If you subordinate yourself to collectives, you will lose all your power. If you ignore collectives, you will ultimately lose your power; no one can exercise any power in a vacuum. The eighth step prevents this fate by addressing not only the impact collective organizations have on us but also the impact that we in turn can have on collective organizations. Our personal credibility and authenticity are on the line when we deal with other people. Professor Laura Roberts of Harvard University, commenting on how we manage other people's impressions of us, said that "When you present yourself in a manner that is both true to self and valued and believed by others, impression management can yield a host of favorable outcomes for you, your team, and your organization."[1]

The Paradox of Choice

When I coach professional business people, I'm struck by how many of them don't feel like they are in charge of their fate. They live on a treadmill, going in a direction they can do little about. Their lives run around a timetable, work, the family, and everything else except themselves. Chasing around all the time, with their long working days, and not feeling in control. That is the reality that many people live by.

But why should it be like this? Despite economic setbacks, Western economies remain affluent overall. Innovations in technology have made our lives better. Goods that were considered luxuries 25 years ago, like computers and satellite TV, are now standard. We have, on the face of it, more scope to live the life we want than our parents or grandparents could conceive of. We have never had so much opportunity to take power and do what we want. So, what is going on?

Part of the answer to this conundrum is that we haven't come to terms with how collective organizations bind us. That's why many of us live lives of quiet desperation. For example, with the invention of the smartphone or iPhone, we can send and receive messages and access the Internet wherever we are. How liberating is that? We could even do our work while lying on a beach.

In that last sentence, you have the conundrum. Businesses now expect employees and associates to continue working even when not in the office. You may leave the office, but you can't leave work. Mobile phones and tablet PCs are like a ball and chain, as work invades personal life. It's hardly a case of *love what you do* as the Blackberry advert a few years ago used to talk about. The result is a failure of many people to own their own life despite the plethora of lifestyle choices we apparently have. We could choose more leisure, perhaps live in a smaller house, work part time, and so on. How much of what we have do we really need? Do we really need three holidays a year? Two cars? A second home? Do we need to keep up with our neighbors? Do we need all the technology we now have access to? We have never had this much opportunity to shape our own lives, and yet we behave as if we have no choice. We don't reconcile the organizational and societal desire for compliance with our own desires for ourselves. What a waste of our own power, just given away!

We face this paradox around lifestyle versus treadmill. No wonder there is an epidemic of depressive illness in the Western world as I write these words. No wonder the midlife crisis can now start as early as the late 20s for some people.

I see a similar crisis playing out in the workplace. I have coached hundreds of people on their future career goals in recent years, where it has become clear that they largely sleepwalked into the career they are in. When I ask them "how did you come to be doing what you do," managers and professionals either *fell* into the career path they are on, or their employer simply told them what to do next. They didn't seem to think they were involved in the decision!

Many people sacrifice themselves to ingratiate other people at work, usually their managers. This sacrifice can happen before we even begin the job! For example, one study reported that, when applying for a job, résumés or curricula vitae that were accompanied with an ingratiating cover letter were rated more highly than applications without any ingratiating information.[2]

The Drain of Conformity

All organizations that we belong to have rules that govern what is OK and what is not OK. In society's case, they are laws. Additionally, work organizations have a softer set of rules, or the way they do things. This would include their cultures, standards of behavior, and codes of conduct. Often, these organizational rules are unwritten. We discover them in their breach, and then of course, we are in potential difficulty.

These rules (written and unwritten) have one main purpose, and that is to generate some sort of conformity from its members. In other words, the aim is to engender compliance. These rules might be imposed on us without our consent, or they may be introduced in our name (with or without consent). Either way, the expectation is compliance, and a breach will be subject to some sort of penalty: –imprisonment, dismissal, expulsion, ostracism, warnings, criticism, being ignored, or whatever.

Collectives tend to reward conformity rather than difference, apart from a few special cases. For instance, children at school who get bullied usually suffer because in some way they are seen as different. Fashion is about conformity, not about being different. There are very strong pressures to conform, even in trivial matters. Let me give an example. Let's say someone in a work meeting makes a proposal that you think is crazy. But the first three people at the meeting all speak in support of it. How easy is it for someone now to oppose it? Not very easy, is the obvious answer. And that's just a trivial example.

Organizations are powerful systems in themselves, and we often feel a pressure to conform. We may even actually want to conform. Of course, a few serial rebels may decide to take on authority, but most of us conform.

There are powerful forces in any group or collective of people, and we must recognize this. However, if we want to be an ethically powerful human being, it means that conformity may not always be the thing to do. When conformity is not the thing, this is the step to ethical power that we bring into play.

Inducing Fear

Having rules and penalties for noncompliance are not the only thing that organizations use. Another tactic used is to emphasize outside threats to the organization itself. For evidence of this, look no further than our society. If it isn't the war on terror, it's trade wars or North Korea. The raising of one external threat after another has one major benefit to any organization; it encourages everyone to conform, often to unpleasant plans. We all submit nowadays to searches at airports that would have been viewed as a serious infringement of personal liberty just 20 years ago, for example. People who are in fear are more likely to conform; fear is a disempowering emotion.

Similarly, businesses emphasize the competition, new technology, and place great emphasis on external threats. This justifies making changes at work, particularly changes that many employees would otherwise see as unpalatable.

It's a funny thing when change is about to hit an organization. It all goes quiet, everybody works in denial of what's about to happen, and the managers adopt a low profile and stop asking you for things. It's a bit like a tree full of birds when a bird of prey approaches. Everything goes quiet, each bird hoping not to be dinner, until the bird of prey strikes, and the impact of change hits us.

Deference to Authority

I believe most of us see little opportunity to influence the society we live in. Most of us conform to the law in a very subservient manner. I had an early experience with authority, when I was caught as a teenager while crossing a railway line, by the British Transport Police. My personal details were taken, and I was told to expect a visit to my parents, so I might as well tell them what I'd done. True to their word, they did turn up and told my parents what I did, and I remember a long and uncomfortable conversation taking place. At least I could give a sigh of relief at the end; matter closed, even if my parents were not pleased with me.

Alas, the matter was not closed. I received a summons out of the blue to appear in court, charged with trespassing. Suddenly, I was a court hearing away from having a criminal record. My heart sank, and I dreaded what might happen. I was thankful to my parents for supporting me on this, and I think they saw it all as an overreaction from the authorities. I appeared in court that day, dressed in school uniform, while the case was argued. In the end, I got let off; no criminal record. I remember the relief of it all, even if the judge made me stand up and receive a dressing down in public; *I never want to see your face in this court again.*

There are people who will see this as a case of serves you right for trespassing, and there's no harm in you getting a scare so you understand right from wrong. But I see it as a huge overreaction to what wasn't much of an offence in the first place, compared to what other people who habitually break the law get away with. The Transport Police talking to my parents did that job; the exercise of a state sledgehammer to crack a nut was simply an invitation for me to make myself subservient to the state, which I did.

Go Chop Your Sleeves Off!

Truly creative people, the ones who made the big differences in the world, are not conformists and that goes whatever the field they were in. Bill Gates, Mother Teresa, Mark Zuckerberg, Bob Geldof, Elvis Presley, and Sir Richard Branson were all nonconformist, at least to some extent. The conformists do not set fashion. It's the people who chop the sleeves off an outfit and then do something else with the bottom half of it that creates change in our lives. Six months later, everyone else is wearing the same outfit. It is nonconformists that are the truly powerful individuals.

I'm not suggesting that we all become nonconformists for the sake of it. I am suggesting that, where it matters to you, you make your stand in life for who you are and what you believe in. Are there some parts of your life where nonconformity could serve you better? Where this is the case, go chop your sleeves off!

That's what the eighth step to ethical power is all about.

The Keys to Success

This gives rise to a good question; what's the point of trying to change things, given the power of collective organizations? Why not just throw in the towel and vote for the winner?

The answer is that it's too costly to not try. You end up feeling bad about yourself. Look at how many people suffer from depression. Look at all the midlife crises that occur now at all stages of life. Look at the suicide levels among the young. Look at all those middle-aged people living their lives of quiet desperation. Simply subordinating yourself to social trends will not give you the life you want.

So, what will help in this situation? There are three keys to success with the eighth step to ethical power. These are awareness, authenticity, and assumptions. Let me say a bit more about each of these three A's.

Awareness

The first is simply to be aware of the power of the collectives you interact with. Then you can decide what to do from a position of knowing rather than ignorance. It's a bit like the first step to ethical power, where you recognized that power is an inevitable fact of life.

Authenticity

Secondly, there's the importance of being authentic, being true to yourself. You know how important it is to live your life in alignment with your purpose and personal values. Sometimes it's important to not only be authentic but also courageous; truly successful people take no notice of the need for conformity where it matters to them. They don't bother how they look compared to other people. They see no need to conform to other people's expectations. As we saw with the sleeves, fashion is set ultimately by the nonconformists. Were it not for nonconformists, nothing would ever change.

Assumptions

We need to learn to recognize the assumptions we make in life. We should also be careful not to assume too much. Let's illustrate this point with an example of a fruitless marriage that's going nowhere. Let's say the husband thinks to himself:

"I want out of this marriage. But if I tell her, I might hurt her feelings. I don't want to do that, so I'll keep quiet."

At the same time, the wife thinks:

"I want out of this marriage. But if I tell him, I might upset him. I don't want to do that. I won't say anything."

What do you think would happen?

The most likely outcome is that neither of them would say anything, meaning neither of them would get what they really wanted. Imagine being in a marriage for 30 years, before you both found out that the other had wanted out for most of that time. You can just imagine the devastation. What a waste of two lives. Yet we all make assumptions along the lines of "if I say or do that in this group, they won't like it, and something unpleasant will happen as a result."

All I want to say here is don't assume how other people will react, unless you really do know. Sometimes what we imagine is much worse than what would actually happen, particularly when we get stressed. It's a bit like our limiting beliefs, and that Henry Ford quote about whether you believe the outcome will be good or not. Our belief will become a self-fulfilling prophecy.

Exercise: My Challenge Now

Think about a challenge where your heart or gut is telling you to make a stand, faced with an authority more powerful than you are. Write down your answers to the following questions.

1. What is the situation?
2. Who else is involved?
3. Who is in authority in this situation? (The assumption is it isn't you, but someone else!)
4. What would your natural default response be in this situation? (fight, flight, freeze)
5. What result do you want to achieve here?
6. Given your desire for self-empowerment, what are you going to say and do?

When completing this exercise, you might want to refer to the following sections for further guidance, especially if the action you are thinking about leaves you feeling uncomfortable.

- Chapter 5 on limiting beliefs, if you think there may be a limiting belief holding you back in this situation, and
- Chapter 9 on being powerful and being rational. This will help you work out how to say what you want to say.

What We Seek from Collectives

Some of the power that collectives hold over us lies in the things we seek from being part of them. Self-determination theory (SDT), first proposed by Deci and Ryan,[3] highlighted that individuals tend to pursue three motivators or needs: autonomy, competence, and relatedness. These motivators were seen as inherent in all human beings. Conditions in work organizations that foster these motivators in people will tend to bring out increased engagement, enhanced performance, greater persistence, and creativity. By contrast, organizations that are not conducive to the promotion of autonomy, competence and relatedness might result in dysfunctional, stressed employees. To quote one source:

> To the extent that the needs are ongoingly satisfied, people will develop and function effectively and experience wellness, but to the extent that they are thwarted, people will more likely evidence ill-being and non-optimal functioning.[4]

Recognizing the power of the collective over us is therefore essential.

Clearly, the more we can generate these motivators intrinsically for ourselves, the more able we are to make meaningful choices in organizational life. However, the more we rely on work organizations to provide us with these motivators, the more reliant and compliant in pursuit of them we are likely to become.

More recent evidence of what motivates people in the workplace comes from David Rock in 2009. We first referred to his SCARF model in Chapter 5, when we talked about the different ways we seek to retain a degree of security. Rock refers to the motivation that drives our social behavior as being driven by the need to maximize rewards and minimize threats. His research highlighted five drivers that motivate us, some of which are similar to SDT. As previously mentioned, the five drivers are as follows:

- *Status*: Our relative importance to other people, our place in the pecking order.
- *Certainty*: The extent to which we can predict the future, particularly the near future.
- *Autonomy*: Our sense of control over events, the space within which we can make our own decisions.
- *Relatedness*: The degree to which we are among friends, people who are friendly toward us, and not hostile.
- *Fairness*: The perception we have that things are being done fairly. The principle of fairness is extended to other people as well as oneself.

Once again, the extent to which we feel threatened by the loss of our motivations at work will reduce our overall sense of well-being as well as inhibit our problem solving and creativity.[5]

Exercise: What Do I Seek from Organizations?

For self-awareness purposes, understanding our own motivations in a social (collective) setting matters if we are to operate effectively within them and retain our own power. Taking both SDT and the SCARF model, what do you look for?

1. Of the above motivators, which ones are particularly strong in your case? You may wish to take a fresh look at this or review your SCARF model answers in Chapter 5.
2. What happens to your performance if these motivators are placed under threat or removed? How does this impact on your power?
3. What steps could you take to become more self-sufficient in generating some of this motivation for yourself and reduce your dependence on organizations to generate it?

Summary

In this chapter, we have explored the eighth step to ethical power, which is about the balance between being an individual and being part of a larger collective of people. Collectives have rules and power structures, and we need to recognize what they are, but not let them cramp our own unique individuality and style if we want to remain in a state of empowerment.

That leaves one final step on the road to ethical power, and in this step, the word ethical comes even more clearly to the fore. While we have talked at times about the importance of maintaining an ethical stance in using our power, the emphasis in most of what we have done to date has been on the power element. However, the final step is primarily about the ethical component. It is to this that we now turn.

CHAPTER 11

Using Power Ethically

As we look ahead into the next century, leaders will be those who empower others.

—*Bill Gates*

The ninth step to ethical power–Use power ethically

The ninth step to ethical power is to use power ethically. Be empathic to other people's circumstances, and avoid manipulating them, which is self-defeating anyway. Recognize the role of trauma in others and the impact on their approach to power. Learning to forgive others and to deal with our own past trauma is important, when confronting people who are negative, overbearing, or manipulative.

Introduction

Consider the following account, from a conference delegate, about a lunch conversation he was involved in:

At lunchtime, a fellow delegate tried to make conversation with me. She introduced herself as Sally and uttered the memorable opening line of "you look like you've got something to think about." Talk about the blatantly obvious. She worked for somebody like Scaline Financial Planning and was the risk assessment manager. RAM eh? These TLAs are brilliant; three letter acronyms, that is. At least RAM is a better one to have than the business unit manager I was introduced to about a

(Continued)

month ago. I struggled not to laugh that day. Anyway, to be honest, I went for minimal compliance with Sally, give some eye contact, nod and grunt when she was talking, and say as little as I could get away with to be polite.

All the while, my mind was elsewhere. Elsewhere as Sally banged on about the latest reality TV controversy that made the news on breakfast TV this morning, no doubt some ex–U.S. President rigging the televised phone vote or something. Elsewhere as Sally picked over the corpse of the morning's conference presentations. Elsewhere as Sally told me her career life story, and what a great place she was working for right now. Elsewhere as Sally talked about how many people she knew who were reexamining their lives, and how she believed in always living each day as if it could be your last.

Poor Sally may have been talking, but she was not being listened to. She was talking to someone who was basically ignoring her. Our conference delegate may have been *polite* about it, but they were engaged to the minimum they thought they could get away with. That isn't engaging behavior, is it? We all know when we talk to someone if they aren't really listening to us. Sally was investing energy into the conversation, and our conference delegate was not. Remember the link between power and energy?

It's safe to assume that the above behavior does *not* represent the ninth step to ethical power in action! It represents what happens when the ninth step is not present.

The ninth step is the step that deals most explicitly with the ethical dimension. This lesson will help you with your manager, work colleagues, friends, family, and everyone you meet.

Most people I meet say that they are committed to using their power ethically. The trouble is there's a difference between aspiring to do it and achieving it. The ninth step explicitly addresses that gap.

We all have the capacity to empathize with other people. We find it easier to empathize with others when certain criteria are satisfied. It's easier when someone needs help, when we get on well with them, when they've done us favors in the past, or when we already have an established relationship with them. In these cases, we will view the world through their eyes and understand their situation whatever it is. It is that quality of viewing the world through the eyes of someone else that is the basis for empathizing.

However, there are three types of challenging character that are harder to empathize with naturally. The first type is the *glass half empty* type. They have a negative outlook on the world and will look for the dark side in human motives. If someone does them a favor, they will be looking for the ulterior motive behind it; what do they want from me? The impact of the glass half empty type is to drain your energy reserves. They gain their energy directly by draining yours, in line with the law of resonance we talked about in Chapter 4.

The second type that is difficult to empathize with is the overbearing type. The person who wants you to do everything for them, be everything to them, go everywhere for them. They are dictatorial and are often very good at using the *be powerful* techniques we talked about in Chapter 9. The trouble is they use it all the time, not just sparingly. They also use it in a way that undermines your power, and they are unlikely to be using the technique legitimately.

The third type is the manipulative type. The manipulator is someone who doesn't say it as it is. They don't tell us what they mean, or they put on an act to avoid showing us how they really feel. They might hope you get the drift from their behavior. When what you say or do isn't how you think or feel, then you are at risk of manipulating others. We will, of course, know when we're being manipulated if we follow the second step to ethical power, as our own feelings in the moment will tell us.

But what do we do when faced with these three types to remain empathic to them. Should we even be empathic? It may not be easy to do so, but the ninth step to ethical power would answer yes to this question. The next question is how do we remain empathic? Genuine empathy is crucial, as opposed to faking it, which is a manipulating tactic in reverse. Other people will, of course, spot fake empathy from a mile away, in the same way that we probably would.

There are three key steps to take that will help us to stay empathic, no matter how difficult the other person is. We will go on to look at these later. But first, let's look at each of the three difficult types in more detail.

How Power Is Abused: Negativity

The first type that can be difficult to deal with are the negative types. Cynicism and negativity are a manipulation of power too. Some people are negative if they want others to feel sorry for them. The negative approach as a tactic has the effect of draining your power. On the face of it, you can do two things with a negative person, assuming you don't just want to tolerate it. Your first option is to tell them about their behavior and its impact on you, in the same way we talked about in the lesson on undressing power (Chapter 8). The second option is to move away from them. I know people who have simply adopted a strategy of minimizing their association with negative types. Only you can decide which option is the best one for you.

You might want to keep an open mind; what is it that fuels the negativity? It takes a lot of energy to stay negative all the time, which suggests that something might lie behind all this negativity. Adopting an approach of unconditional regard for others can be helpful, accepting that most people are trying to do their best with the resources they have. The results may not look very good, but it's true nonetheless. It helps to show empathy and to feel unconditional regard. That helps people to feel they can be open with you if they need to, especially if you'd like them to change their behavior.

The antidote with the negative type is simply to take steps to ensure that they don't have the impact of draining your power. In other words, don't let their negativity drain your positivity (and I hope you are developing a sense of positivity by now!). If you remain positive in the face of this, the negative person may simply decide to move away from you.

How Power Is Abused: Overbearing

Another word for overbearing is aggressive. We've all met this type before, for whom everything is a battle and they must win it. Of course, their winning in the battle means you end up losing it. The difference between this type and the manipulative type is that there is no deception involved. You are not so much being wrong-footed as overpowered. It may be that they use the be powerful style so often that they give the message that they are more important than you are and you do not have any rights.

I used to have a manager who was this type. Sitting in the same office as her for any length of time felt like sitting exposed to continual machine gun fire!

The temptation with the overbearing type will be to do one of two things. The first option is to fight back, to be rational, and be powerful in return. But if this is the only tactic you use, the result is likely to be ongoing conflict. The second option is to accommodate the person and back down. But this, if it's all you do, means you are in a disempowered position whenever you are faced with this person.

There may be situations where you do one of the above. You stand up for yourself if the issue matters to you. You accommodate the other person if the issue doesn't matter as much. But the other part of this is that you remain empathic to the other person's situation and listen to them. Remember, to empathize with them is not to agree with them. But it is to understand them, and understanding is priceless to the quality of a relationship.

How Power Is Abused: Manipulation

Most people usually intend to be helpful. They don't intend to manipulate other people's power. But what about people who do? What incentive do they have to change? They might modify their behavior toward me if I challenge them more. But won't they just go and manipulate someone else instead?

That's a good question. To a degree, most of us manipulate other people now and again. However, there are people out there who serially manipulate or bully others.

The first thing to say is that most bullies are not bullies all the time. For example, the workplace bully might be bullied or manipulated at home by someone else. Often bullies in one sphere of life are under the thumb in other parts of their life. You just don't know.

Let me give you an example of a guy I once knew to illustrate why the lessons in this book apply just as much to the overpowerful as to the under powerful. Alan was a manipulative character who put other people down, from close relatives to work colleagues. He justified it by saying that if you want to get to the top, you need to clamber on top of everyone else. In his view, life was dog-eat-dog.

He was on the face of it very successful, even if he was never satisfied with life. There was always someone or something wrong, that needed sorting. Then, in his late 30s, he had a heart attack. He survived, but this shook him up enough for him to realize there must be more to life than the cycle he was currently on. As a result, he made some major changes to his life, which resulted in a move from the world of high business onto the board of a major national charity. He also started to dabble in the world of spirituality and read books on religion and new age thinking.

Sounds like he made some positive changes to his life then? Maybe. That's not what happened though. Basically, his wife ended up leaving him, and his daughter left home vowing never to speak to him again. In the end, he had a breakdown and ended up in psychiatric therapy after he'd lost control of his life. Not the ending I'd have expected for someone changing his life in this way and working hard for charity. But consider this; for all the changes Alan made, he didn't change his approach to power. He continued to manipulate other people in pursuit of his personal and career goals, even if they were now more altruistic goals. It was a bit like the Machiavellian philosophy about how the end can justify the means.[1] Alan behaved as if this was the case.

The ends were more altruistic, but his means were still not justifiable. The result was that he alienated all the people around him, ignored and put upon his family, and fell apart when things at his charity went wrong. In short, he didn't learn to share power, or to help other people build theirs up. He did charitable work because he made himself feel good, not because he helped other people feel better. He learned a tough lesson. The shame in all this was that he thought he was trying his best for other people. His testimony of what happened next is as follows:

> Yes, I abused other people's power. I ignored their feelings, always justifying it to myself. I knew what was best for my daughter, more than she did. I took my wife for granted and undermined her sense of self-worth. I didn't listen to my colleagues in the charity. I always wanted more and more, faster and faster. It was only when I realized how destructive my attitude to power and other people was that I changed my approach and became the wonderful man you see now! But I lost everything before I made the

change. It was too late to save my marriage, although I've made my peace with my daughter.

Getting your power balance right is important. Balancing your power against those around you, and not allowing what you think are good ends to justify bad means, is important. The widely used exhortation that we should be the change we wish to see in the world is good advice.[2]

We all manipulate other people to some extent. After all, we are human, and we learn techniques and strategies from childhood to get what we want. Some of these are backdoor strategies, which are manipulative in character. Once we become aware of these strategies and tactics, we can do something to change them, and we become more aligned with ethical power.

Remember, whenever what you say isn't what you mean, and you cover up your true feelings and intentions, you are to some extent being manipulative toward other people.

You now have the opportunity to do some self-reflection, on your own manipulative tactics of choice, and to consider how you might change your behavior with the difficult types we talked about earlier.

Exercise: My Manipulation of Others

Consider a situation from the past where, on reflection, you manipulated another person in an attempt to gain a result. Try to answer the following questions:

1. Describe the situation?
2. What was the result you really wanted but didn't reveal?
3. In what ways did you manipulate and with whom?
4. What happened as a result? Comment on both the result achieved and the impact on your relationship with this other person.
5. How would you deal with it if this situation were to arise again?

Consider the type of manipulation you used in this example. Where did you first learn to do this? Did you learn it from someone else? Or did you try it and gain a good result in the past?

Exercise: How Can I Change Things?

For this exercise, I'd like you to think about the three difficult types outlined above, which are:

- The negative type
- The overbearing type
- The manipulative type

I'm going to ask you to think about someone you find it hard to get on with for one of the above three reasons. This is a chance to think about how you can modify your behavior to be more ethical in this situation and perhaps to influence the other person's behavior for the better.

1. Describe the situation and the other person; what type are they?
2. How do you currently behave with them?
3. How could you change your behavior?
   a. To become more empathetic?
   b. To protect yourself from their impact on you?
4. More generally, consider which of the three types you find it most difficult to get along with. What is it that makes them the biggest challenge for you?

How We Rationalize Disempowering Others

Consulting with people is a good way of reducing the risk that you'll end up abusing their power. If you're thinking about doing something that affects someone else, and you aren't telling them about it, it's worth asking yourself why you're not telling them. The answer will say a lot about whether you risk abusing their power.

But can't some of these justifications be valid sometimes? Ah, I used the word justification, didn't I? That leads me to another point, the difference between a justification and an explanation.

An explanation aims to clarify something or to make it understandable. A justification has an additional bit to it, in that it attempts to justify or defend something. The problem is that people often confuse these things. So, to give an obvious example, let me give you an explanation of Adolf Hitler's rise to power in Germany during the 1930s.

Hitler's rise was due to a variety of factors. The poverty in Germany in the 1920s and 1930s along with the effects of the Great Depression were key factors, generating discontent that subsequently became nationalistic in nature. The humiliation of Germany at the end of World War I, and the desire of many Germans to feel good about their country again, further contributed to Hitler's rise. The Nazi Party's ability to tap into anti-Semitism that was rife in Europe helped their cause. Finally, the weakness of the other European powers at the time like Britain and France, and the fear of communism allowed Hitler space and time to fuel his expansion. I could continue this analysis, but all these factors explain Hitler's rise to power. He was also a magnetic public speaker and aroused emotion in a way few other leaders of his time did.[3]

As an explanation for the rise of Adolf Hitler, I've probably given a reasonable one. However, I cannot justify his rise. The man was evil. I can explain it, but not justify it.

In this extreme case, the difference is clear. It's less clear in other cases. For instance, I clearly remember an example where a client explained why it was that they were unable to confront their manager over how she treated him. His reasoning was that, if he did confront her, he might lose his job. That was a great explanation of his predicament. But how good a justification was it? Arguably, it wasn't a very good one. But, in his eyes, he was attempting to justify his decision to avoid confronting her at that point.

This confusion between explanation and justification does not help when it comes to power. We confuse these concepts from an early age. How often do you hear children say things like "I only did this because he did whatever" to someone or other? I certainly said that when I was young. Then adults say things like "I'm only saying this, so I can help you do it better" or "that's just the type of person I am." This is the same behavior, is it not?

Always keep your ears open for this confusion and check when you go into an explanation that you're not just trying to justify something by the back door. The effect of doing this often is very manipulative and saps the power of others.

So, you can listen to yourself, what you say, and check your own motive. Can you do anything else to check your own inclination at times to manipulate other people?

Consequences of Unethical Power

You might choose to say "well, I am a powerful person; what does it matter if my ethics are a bit curtailed at some points? Does it really matter?" I would argue that it does, and there are some significant consequences of not choosing to follow this step to ethical power. Here are three of the key ones.

1. *Getting somewhere will depend solely on your own power*
   Other people won't help you unless they must, and that will depend on your power over them. You will probably end up relying on your reward, coercive, and expert power sources, as described in Chapter 3. Should you lose these sources, you will end up in trouble.
2. *You can't fool all the people all the time*
   To be blunt, people will eventually see through you, no matter how skilled you think you might be. Once they have seen through you, you've lost the ability to manipulate them, and you have lost their goodwill too.
3. *You end up on your own*
   Pursuit of power without ethics destroys relationships. You cannot make people like you, even if they must deal with you. There are many examples of senior managers, used to having things their own way, who when they retire find they have no friends to talk to. Once your previous power sources have gone, you have very little else you can fall back on if you haven't developed the ethical dimension.

∞

Pursuing ethical power is not only the moral thing to do, it is the only long-term effective approach there is. Most of us will own up to wanting to achieve things in our life and work (albeit some will want to achieve more than others). Most of us will own up to wanting at least some productive, close, trusting, friendly, and loving relationships. If we want both things, the pursuit of ethical power is the only viable option.

The Organizational Imperative

The importance of ethical behavior in business is becoming more important by the day. There is much attention around how employees, customers, and stakeholders are treated in business. From tackling bullying and harassment to data protection, confidential information, and consumer rights, how we treat people in business is both important in itself and critical to a good corporate image.

Key to being ethical is the point that it's not just what you do, it's the way that you do it. In particular, to return to the Machiavelli misquotation earlier in this chapter, the end does not justify the means. It is better to treat people as an end in themselves, not just as a means to an end. Let's face it, none of us want to be treated as the means to someone else's end. So why would anyone else be different from this? If we want other people to treat us the way we want to be treated, then it is incumbent on us to treat other people the way they want to be treated.

Most organizations now incorporate statements around business ethics, including principles on how we should behave in the workplace. Values statements and behavioral competency structures in many businesses set out how we should individually behave in the workplace. In my 30-year career to date, I have lost count of the number of times I've heard the organizational mantra stated that "people are our most important asset."

I'm not sure if that's what I want to be, an asset? But, leaving that to one side, how many businesses really do treat people as their most important asset? Are we more important than financial assets? Property? Intellectual assets? Clearly, many organizations do not match up to their statement on the importance of people.

Other stakeholders at times fare little better, including customers. For example, the Royal Bank of Scotland (RBS) was recently accused of pushing struggling UK small-to-medium businesses into a "turnaround division," which led to higher banking charges and selling off of business assets. This generated significant profit for RBS via a scheme known as "project dash for cash." Criteria for businesses being placed in the turn-around division included the customer falling out with the bank in some way![4]

We all know that it isn't enough to parrot statements about the impor-tance of ethics, behaviors, and values. Backing them up with real ethical behavior is vital too. The failure of Enron in 2001, widely documented, highlights the irony for a business that claimed to promote respect, integ-rity, communication, and excellence in the way it behaved. As investiga-tions showed, in practice Enron behaved nothing like this.

According to Dacher Keltner, people tend to look for social intelli-gence from their business leaders. With social intelligence comes modesty and empathy. However, these tend to be the very qualities that are dam-aged by the experience of holding formal power over other people. In one telling passage, he goes on to explain:

> studies also show that once people assume positions of power, they're likely to act more selfishly, impulsively, and aggressively, and they have a harder time seeing the world from other people's points of view. This presents us with the paradox of power.[5]

The seat of ethical power lies in the appropriate use of referent power. It is the source of power that is positively related to a number of key organizational indicators of employee satisfaction, which include quality of supervision, organizational commitment, and employee performance.[6]

Doing the right thing because it is the right thing to do is good business. In the long term, it will create a more profitable, sustainable business, with more motivated employees. Clearly then, effective organ-izations need people who exercise ethical power, and the ninth step is critical to this.

Ethical Power Strategies

Being empathic, and asking other people what they think, will help you to remain ethically powerful. People watching is a key skill if you want to be empathic with other people. What do you think you might see if you're switching someone off or in some way undermining their power? Some of the signs might be obvious ones. They may stop looking at you, so there is no eye contact. They might fold their arms. They might shrink in their chairs or slouch if standing. They may even look angry or agitated if they decide they really don't like what you're saying or doing.

People who've been disempowered will often lose their color and turn gray; life is literally drained out of them. So, keep an eye out for the energy flows in other people, and you will see when you are literally switching them off.

There are three key ethical power strategies that I want to focus on that will make a huge difference to your achievement of Step 9 on the road to ethical power. They are:

1. Recognizing the impact of traumatic events on others and ourselves.
2. Cultivating the art of forgiveness.
3. Avoiding manipulation as a tactic of choice.

The Impact of Trauma

We all have our histories, and they affect us. One of the things we all have at some point in life is trauma. Some face greater tragedy, while other bad events can be expected, like the eventual death of parents. But, whatever it is, traumatic events will affect us. If we don't or can't deal with them, then they will affect our approach to life, work, other people, and to power. If we don't come to terms with our traumas, they will sit there, eating away at us, and undermining the rest of our life.

As it is with us, so it is with others. It is important that we cut people some slack when they behave badly. It may simply reflect traumatic events they haven't come to terms with. Ample doses of empathy, listening, and unconditional positive regard are a good start to this. We should stay empathic to their life circumstances. Recognize that they will have felt disappointment, rejection, hurt, and possibly trauma. It may be that what traumatized them would not have traumatized you, but that is not the point. Trauma is personal; it is the impact of an event on a person at a point in time. Other people may not see what we've been through as traumatic either.

Challenging characters are just like the rest of us. Their ways of behaving are how they try to cover up their past adversities and to prevent them from happening again. It's just that their specific tactics are harder for you to deal with, perhaps reflecting the trauma they have been through. Recognizing this fact may help you to empathize more with them.

I would encourage you to look at your own past for evidence on how you behave currently, where that behavior causes difficulties for other people you know at home, at work, or anywhere else.

By understanding our own traumas, what contributed to them, and their impact on our current behavior, we can develop our empathy toward other people and the traumas they may have faced.

Exercise: My Trauma

1. Describe a behavior you have that one or more people find difficult to deal with. You may have received feedback on it from others in the past. In any event, you are aware of this behavior.
2. What past event triggered this behavior for you? Think back to when you first became aware of it. What was it an attempt to resolve?
3. What negative belief (about yourself or other people) lies behind your behavior now?
4. How could you change your behavior to deliver a more constructive outcome?

The Art of Forgiveness

The trouble with trauma is that, usually, something or someone can be held responsible for what happened—whether or not they were responsible. It's important to learn to forgive and to stop blaming. Nonforgiveness destroys our own power by tying up our energy reserves in a negative blame game. That energy then can't be used for more constructive pursuits. So, learning to forgive is crucial, forgiving ourselves and other people as appropriate. Failure to forgive means continuing to tie up energy in fighting the fight that you cannot resolve and don't move on from. Learning to forgive is the single biggest thing we can do to raise our own power.

We've all met people who don't find forgiveness easy. They go around in life collecting scores to settle, of people who wronged them at some point in the past. They may self-righteously take every opportunity to rub other people's noses in it, reminding them of what they did, or fall out with people all the time. We've all met people at work who spend all their time looking angry or irritable, just waiting for the next conflict.

But there's another type of nonforgiveness. This is the person who can't forgive themselves for things they may have done in the past. Instead of beating other people up, they choose to beat themselves up. For example, one of the most difficult things I had to forgive myself for was for the way that I ended my first marriage. That took a while, but I realized that until I did, I would never summon up enough energy to move on and rebuild my life.

Whether it's others or ourselves that we fail to forgive, the result is the same from a power perspective. The impact in either case is primarily on ourselves. When we don't forgive, we tie our own energy up inside ourselves. Instead of forgiving others, we fight past battles, imagining what we'd say to the other people involved if we could. When we beat ourselves up over the things we cannot change, similarly the energy tied up is lost to today, preventing us from doing something productive with it now.

Let me be clear that forgiveness is not simply forgetting about the past—there are valuable lessons we can learn. Nor is forgiveness about letting other people off the hook, for example, if there's still stuff to be said. It's about letting go of that knot in energy that binds us up to the past. Forgiveness releases this energy, and once released, we can choose to use it more constructively.

The "Sorry" Myth

Many people I've known and worked with have taken the view that "I would forgive them if only they would say sorry," or alternatively "I've apologized to them, why won't they forgive me?" These are both valid points to make, and they deserve an answer.

Here then is my answer. The word *sorry* is utterly irrelevant to forgiveness! Does that sound strange? This is why I say that. With the first point, why on earth are you tying your own energy in knots waiting for someone else to say sorry? All you're doing is harming yourself, and what's the point of that? If the other person chooses not to say sorry, that's their problem—why are you compounding the original sin by continuing to invest in it? This is a futile activity, and you are better off letting go. Indeed, if the other person knows you're waiting for an apology before letting go, they might refuse to give one just to keep you on the hook! The best course of action is to let it go. You don't have to tell them you forgive them, but if you do forgive them, you remove the power they have over you. You also defuse all your emotion for the other person. That leaves you free to move away from them should you choose.

On the other hand, if you've apologized to them genuinely, and they don't forgive you, that's their problem. All they are doing is harming themselves, and it's up to them to stop doing this. Of course, again they may be refusing to forgive as a tactic to keep you under their power. Don't connive in that game. Just take yourself somewhere else instead.

Exercise: Who Do I Forgive?

In this exercise, I'd like you to consider your approach to forgiveness. For each statement below, some telltale signs of a lack of forgiveness are covered. To what extent, do you display each characteristic? It is important to be honest with yourself.

Part 1: Forgiving Others
1. I take a long time to forget other people's transgressions against me; for example, I keep going over them in my mind.
2. I imagine how I might get my own back on people who've done bad things to me.
3. I remind people of the occasions when they've let me down.
4. I talk about people who've let me down to other people.
5. I snap with people on minor transgressions out of proportion to these transgressions, partly because of what they've done to me in the past.

Part 2: Forgiving Self
1. I take a long time to forget my transgressions against other people; for example, I keep going over them in my mind.

2. I imagine how other people might get their own back on me because I've been bad to them.

3. I remind myself of the occasions when I've let other people down.

4. I talk to other people about the times where I've let others down—in other words, I put myself down.

5. I snap with myself on minor transgressions out of proportion to these transgressions, partly because of what I've done in the past.

Now review the above answers. To what extent, do you forgive yourself for things you've done in the past? To what extent, do you forgive others for their transgressions against you? Do you find it harder to forgive others or yourself?

Forgiveness Is for Life

Have you ever seen a situation where a person says they forgive someone else for something they've done previously? Then, something else happened; whether it's a minor or major transgression. The response that the transgressor receives is along the following lines:

"That's just typical of you! How many times does this have to happen? You clearly have no respect for me" and so on.

Let's be honest, that happens quite often. The one thing that's clear to me is that the original sin was not forgiven despite what was said at the time. Instead, it was put away and stored, to be brought out the next time something happens, and it did! True forgiveness means discharging or letting go of the emotion at the time.

Avoid Manipulation as a Tactic of Choice

The third key element in Step 9 on the road to ethical power is to avoid the use of manipulative tactics when dealing with other people. Before we go any further, let me again define what I mean by manipulation.

Manipulation is where we don't say what we mean or where what we do doesn't reflect how we feel. In other words, it is where my talk or behavior is not transparent to other people. For example, by not saying that we feel anger when we do or trying to get something we want by the back door instead of openly saying it.

We all manipulate other people to some extent. For many of us, it is a subconscious process, and consequently we're not aware of when we're doing it. But we can learn to become more aware. We shouldn't beat ourselves up over this; remember the lessons from the forgiveness section above! We will have learned our own manipulating tactics partly as a response to our own life traumas from the past. They are our tactics to get what we want or need and to avoid failure and rejection. Our own individual manipulative programming will run deep within ourselves, largely from childhood.

However, understanding how and why we manipulate does not justify it. When what we say isn't what we mean or what we do isn't how we feel, then we need to find ways to reduce the gap. So, when we have an issue with someone, we should let them know, rather than let it fester, or gossip to other people about it. The moment we stop being open we move toward the world of manipulation. Alternatively, letting them know in an inappropriate way fuels the fires of manipulation, throwing tantrums, sulking, huffing. or ignoring them.

In the end, manipulative behavior destroys relationships. At the very least, it formalizes them. Procedures and processes are introduced to regulate the manipulation. Manipulation is incompatible with having constructive, strong relationships at work or at home.

Avoid manipulation as a tactic of choice in your life. Unless, that is, you think you can happily run your life without meaningful relationships.

The Result of Step 9

A strange thing happens when we learn to forgive and let go, when we challenge our manipulative tactics at times, and when we deal with our trauma while recognizing other people's trauma. In a nutshell, we learn to listen!

It was many years ago that Stephen Covey wrote his book on the seven habits of highly effective people. What were the things that effective business people did that less effective people didn't do, did less often, or did less well? One of these habits was the art of listening.[7]

Covey outlined five levels of listening, from low to high:

Level 1: Ignoring: This is obvious!

Level 2: Pretending: We pretend to listen, but our attention is primarily directed toward something else, like doing some work, watching TV, or eavesdropping in on another conversation. But we keep minimal eye contact, and nod and grunt (often at inappropriate points!) to keep up the pretense of listening.

Level 3: Selective listening: This is the level of listening most of us operate to when we think we are listening, including social conversations. With selective listening, we are either listening for what we want to hear, or we listen for a pause in the conversation, so we can say something really important! Other people, of course, will realize this. To quote Simon and Garfunkel's famous song, "a man hears what he wants to hear and disregards the rest."[8] This is selective listening, listening with our own agenda in mind.

Level 4: Active listening: Here, we are listening with the intention to understand the other person's agenda or point of view. It is at this level that we cease manipulative behavior. We stop giving our opinions and start asking questions to find out more. We become more interested and curious about other people and how they see things. It is at this stage that we are really listening. It takes effort to do this for long periods.

Level 5: Empathetic listening: According to Covey, this is the highest level of listening and is very intensive. At this level, we are picking up on how the person feels as well as what they think. We will also hear what's not being said as well as what is being said; for example, if someone is avoiding talking about a particular issue for some reason.

It is at levels 4 and 5 that we really build connections with other people, which raises another interesting point. Over the last 30 years, I have trained thousands of leaders and managers in business and other work organizations. I often ask delegates to bring to mind someone from their past (or present) who has influenced them greatly during their career, and they have learned from. Then I ask about what it was these role models did that made them so influential. One quality that came through in the vast majority of cases was that they were good listeners. In other words, we are far more influenced by managers and professional people who listen to us than we are by those who don't listen!

The moral of this story is clear; listening well is not only crucial to ethical power, it also gives us real power to influence other human beings. Isn't that what we all want, in business and beyond?

It is true, I believe, that most people yearn to be understood by others. Listening is the only quality that will allow this to happen, and we are in turn influenced heavily by good listeners.

So, we return to Sally at the start of this chapter. She was clearly not listened to by someone who was preoccupied with his own thoughts. That is not a business connection she will want to keep after that conference. But it might have been had listening levels been higher. Listening builds connections, and connections build referent power. Active and empathetic listeners manipulate less, and while we will all slip to selective listening at times, if we learn to recognize this, we can choose to do something about it.

I leave you with one quote from David Rivera, which resonates with me on this topic:

> Whose reality is real? Reality is subjective. Reality is shaped by one's place in the world. To deny a person's reality, is to deny their place in the world.[9]

Summary

In this chapter, we have explored the ninth step to ethical power, which is to use power ethically. Be empathic to other people's circumstances, and avoid manipulating them, which is self-defeating if we want to be influential.

We considered the different types of difficult character that can be hard to empathize with, the negative, overbearing, and manipulative types. We looked at ways to develop our own levels of empathy and forgiveness and to reduce the degree to which we manipulate other people. This will in turn help us to listen to other people more effectively. To the extent that we can achieve these things, we will have adopted ethical power as a foundation for our behavior.

We have now reached the end of the journey to ethical power. We have looked at each of the nine steps and completed a range of personal development and reflective exercises designed to develop your prowess at each of the steps.

To this extent, you have been climbing a staircase while reading this book, with each step constituting another step to ethical power. At any one point, we were concentrating on the current step. This is a good tactic when climbing the staircase, as the last thing we want to do is to fall! However, the other good thing about climbing a staircase is that, when we get to the top, we can admire the view. That is what we'll do next, now that we've completed the staircase to ethical power.

CHAPTER 12

The Clarion Call to Power

If you don't design your own life plan, chances are you'll fall into someone else's plan. And guess what they have planned for you? Not much.

—Jim Rohn

I've always loved the song *Always look on the bright side of life*, at the end of the Monty Python Film *The life of Brian*. Not without controversy when it was launched in 1979, the film pokes fun at the way we take many things so seriously. Among other things, it lampoons the way in which many people are just looking for someone to follow.

At the end of the film is the death scene, after Brian has been crucified, along with others. The victims end up singing "life's a laugh and death's a joke, it's true." Pointing out that life is little more than a show, the song concludes with "just remember that the last laugh is on you."[1]

Ironically, this song has gained a reputation as a feel-good song. However, it also encourages us to think about what life looks like when it's close to the end.

It is equally ironic that we spend so much of our life on this planet playing it safe. Yet clearly life equals risk. Without taking risks at least sometimes, you don't live. Nor do you achieve. I'm not suggesting a bungee jump off the Golden Gate Bridge or that you take up shark-watching as a hobby. But it never ceases to amaze me how people will take a risk in pursuit of a thrill, but then not take one in pursuit of a life.

All this playing it safe is ultimately futile, because one day, we will breathe our last. Will we be pleased at all the times we played it safe and cramped our own power and potential as human beings? Somehow, I doubt it.

If you follow the nine steps in this book, you will become ethically powerful, with all the rewards that go with that. The greatest of which is to feel truly alive and to move toward achieving those things you always wanted to achieve in your career and life. And that is your challenge, so that near the end of your life, you look back with satisfaction at a life full of life rather than with a lifetime of regret and *if only's*. Take the challenge up and take the risk. Without the risk, there is no life.

The following comment is not untypical of someone starting the journey toward empowering themselves:

> I realized that I was a man with a mission, that it was just beginning, and it felt really exciting. I had a career to build, people to see, things to do, friends to help, and a wife and family to rebuild my relationships with. All of this, and yet I felt like I had a blank sheet of paper as well. It's time for the play to begin.

I couldn't put it better than that.

The Nine Steps to Ethical Power

Follow the steps below if you want to become an ethically powerful individual.

Step 1: Accept That Power Is Inevitable

The first step is to recognize power as an inevitable fact of life. Ignoring power doesn't make it go away. It just means you lose influence over your own life, putting it in the hands of others. Recognizing the different types of power can also be helpful.

Step 2: Notice How You Feel in the Moment

The second step is to connect to your feelings in the moment as key to working out whether your power is being exercised or undermined. There are several telltale signs that you are losing your own power. Noticing them will tell you your current state of power, and this is crucial as power is often used and misused subtly.

Step 3: Identify What Trips Your Power Switch

The third step is to identify the things that trip your power switch. Work out the situations where you allow others to take your power or where you disable yourself. Become aware of your own natural response to power, including the childhood responses of fight, flight, and freeze. We take our child response into adulthood, and this can trip us up sometimes. Tackling our negative self-talk is important.

Step 4: Assess Your Current Level of Power

The fourth step is to assess your current level of power by examining each area of your life. The happier you are with an area of your life, the more empowered you are in that area, and vice versa. The more energy you have overall, the less tired you feel, and the more empowered you are.

Step 5: Get Clear on What Matters

The fifth step is to get clear on what matters. Decide what's really important to you, your own purpose and personal values. Being clear about these tells us where we need to exert our personal power. If we have no clear sense of direction, we will always be reacting to other people's agendas rather than setting our own.

Step 6: Undress Power

The sixth step is to undress power. Where you notice other people undermining your power, it's important that you let them know the impact they're having on you, to bring it into the open. Doing this ethically and respectfully will allow other people to change their behavior toward you, without undermining their own power.

Step 7: Redress Power

The seventh step is to use assertive behaviors to build your power base up with others. Be proactive, make decisions, act on them, and take responsibility for them. Recognize that sometimes it may be better to seek forgiveness than to seek permission.

Step 8: Stay Individual and Connected

The eighth step is to remain a powerful individual in the face of the pressures that exist in society, such as the pressure to conform. Being authentic and courageous is key, as well as balancing your own unique individuality with the wider collective needs that exist. Truly powerful, influential people don't just conform to the majority.

Step 9: Use Power Ethically

The ninth step is to use power ethically. Be empathic to other people's circumstances and avoid manipulating them, which is self-defeating anyway. Recognize the role of trauma in others and the impact on their approach to power. Learning to forgive others and to deal with our own past trauma is also important, when confronting people who are negative, overbearing, or manipulative.

Notes

Introduction

1. For one account, visit; Marano, H.E. 2003. "Our Brain's Negative Bias," https://www.psychologytoday.com/articles/200306/our-brains-negative-bias, (accessed March 19, 2018).
2. Williamson, M. 1992. *A Return to Love*. New York, NY: Harper Collins, p. 190.

Chapter 1—Power Scenarios

1. Buber, M. 1947. *Tales of the Hasidim*. New York, NY: Schocken Books.
2. Keltner, D. 2007. "The Power Paradox," *Greater Good Magazine*. https://greatergood.berkeley.edu/article/item/power_paradox, (accessed July 17, 2018).

Chapter 2—The Disempowerment Game

1. Original work is from; Sanford, N. 1966. *Self and Society: Social Change and Individual Development*. New Brunswick, Canada: Transaction Publishers.
2. American Psychiatric Association. 2013. *Diagnostic and Statistical Manual of Mental Disorders (DSM)*. 5th ed. Arlington, VA: American Psychiatric Association, p. 659.
3. Personality Disorders Awareness Network. 2015. "Antisocial Personality Disorder." www.pdan.org/antisocial-personality-disorder, (accessed February 1, 2018).
4. Williams, M.E. 2012. "Brene Brown's Campaign against Snark." www.salon.com/2012/09/18/brene_browns_campaign_against_snark, (accessed March 19, 2018).
5. Keltner, D. 2007. "The Power Paradox," *Greater Good Magazine*. https://greatergood.berkeley.edu/article/item/power_paradox, (accessed July 17, 2018).
6. BusinessDictionary. 2018. "Ethical Behavior Definition." http://www.businessdictionary.com/definition/ethical-behavior.html, (accessed July 17, 2018).

7. Keltner, D. 2007. "The Power Paradox," *Greater Good Magazine*. https://greatergood.berkeley.edu/article/item/power_paradox, (accessed July 17, 2018).

Chapter 3—The Inevitability of Power

1. Peter, L. 1988. *Quotations for Our Time*. London: Maxwell Pergamon Publishing, p. 398.
2. French, J., and Raven, B. 1959. "The Bases of Social Power." In *Studies in Social Power*, ed. D. Cartwright. Ann Arbor, MI: Institute for Social Research, pp. 150–67.
3. Norman Lamont's resignation speech, House of Commons. June 9, 1993. Available at: www.bbc.co.uk. "Norman Lamont Resigns." http://news.bbc.co.uk/democracylive/hi/historic_moments/newsid_8184000/8184411.stm, (accessed February 26, 2018).
4. Six years after the original book, Raven added an additional source of power called Informational power. This is where you have control over information flows other people may get access to, while you yourself have access to significant amounts of information. People who are well-connected have significant information power. However, I have stuck to the original five in the classification, for simplicity and as "Information" could be argued to be implicitly covered by the Expert category.

Chapter 4—Noticing Your Power

1. Wolff, R. 2013. *Capitalism Hits the Fan*. 2nd ed. Northampton, MA: Interlink Books.
2. Jeffers, S. 1991. *Feel the Fear and Do It Anyway*. London, England: Vermilion, p. 192.

Chapter 5—Power Trips

1. Cannon, W.B. 1929. *Bodily Changes in Pain, Hunger, Fear, and Rage*. New York, NY: Appleton-Century-Crofts.
2. Block, P. 2011. *Flawless Consulting*. 3rd ed. San Francisco, CA: Jossey Bass Wiley.
3. First quoted in: *Readers Digest*. September 1947. New York, NY: The Readers Digest Association Inc.
4. Rotter, J.B. 1966. "Generalized Expectations for Internal versus External Control of Reinforcement." *Psychological Monograph* 80, no. 1, pp. 1–28.

5. Jain, A.K., S.I. Giga, and C.L. Cooper. 2009. "Employee Wellbeing, Control and Organizational Commitment." *Leadership & Organization Development* 30, no. 3, pp. 256–73.

6. Adams, L. "Learning a New Skill is Easier Said Than Done," *Gordon Training International*. www.gordontraining.com/free-workplace-articles/learning-a-new-skill-is-easier-said-than-done, (accessed January 19, 2018). The approach was originally attributed to Noel Burch, an employee of GTI.

7. Rock, D. 2008. "SCARF: A Brain-based Model for Collaborating with and Influencing Others." *NeuroLeadership*, no. 1, pp. 1–9.

Chapter 6—Your Current Level of Power

1. Rotter, J.B. 1966. "Generalized Expectations for Internal Versus External Control of reinforcement." *Psychological Monograph* 80, no. 1, pp. 1–28.

2. Dweck, C.S. 2006. *Mindset: The New Psychology of Success*. New York, NY: Random House.

Chapter 7—What Matters?

1. Leider, R. September 15, 2003. Work with a Purpose: Igniting True Engagement in Yourself and Others. Institute of Management Studies seminar, Edinburgh. Richard Leider is founder of The Inventure Group. Available at www.richardleider.com

2. Robbins, A. 2001. *Awaken the Giant Within*. London, England: Simon & Schuster Ltd, pp. 271–308.

3. Kilmann, R.H., and K.W. Thomas. 1977. "Developing a Forced–choice Method of Conflict–handling Behavior: The MODE Instrument." *Educational and Psychological Measurement* 37, no. 2, pp. 309–25.

Chapter 8—Undressing Power

1. Marx, K. [1843] 1970. *A Contribution to the Critique of Hegel's Philosophy of Right*. Cambridge, England: Cambridge University Press.

2. Beckhard, R., and R.T. Harris. 1987. *Organizational Transitions: Understanding Complex Change*. Reading, MA: Addison-Wesley.

3. Block, P. 2011. *Flawless Consulting*. 3rd ed. San Francisco, CA: Jossey Bass Wiley.

Chapter 9—Redressing Power

1. Langer, E., A. Blank, and B. Chanowitz. 1978. "The Mindlessness of Ostensibly Thoughtful Action." *Journal of Personality and Social Psychology* 36, pp. 635–42.
2. Higgins, C.A., T.A. Judge, and G.R. Ferris. 2003. "Influence Tactics and Work Outcomes: A Meta-analysis." *Journal of Organizational Behavior* 24, pp. 89–106.

Chapter 10—Staying Individual and Connected

1. Stark, M. 2005. "Creating a Positive Professional Image. Q&A with Laura Morgan Roberts," *Harvard Business School website*. http://hbswk.hbs.edu/item/4860.html, (accessed July 17, 2018).
2. Varma, A., S.M. Toh, and S. Pichler. 2006. "Ingratiation in Job Applications: Impact on Selection Decisions." *Journal of Managerial Psychology* 21, pp. 200–10.
3. Ryan, R.M., and E.L. Deci. 2000. "Self-determination Theory and the Facilitation of Intrinsic Motivation, Social Development, and Well-being." *American Psychologist* 55, no. 1, p. 68.
4. Self-Determination Theory. 2018. "Theory," http://selfdeterminationtheory.org/theory/, (accessed July 17, 2018).
5. Rock, D. 2008. "SCARF: A Brain-based Model for Collaborating with and Influencing Others." *NeuroLeadership Journal* no. 1.

Chapter 11—Using Power Ethically

1. Ironically, Niccolò Machiavelli never actually used this phrase in his seminal book *The Prince*. He used an altogether subtler line of argument, which some have interpreted as being satirical!
2. This quote is widely attributed to Mohandas Gandhi, but there is no evidence that he said it. In 1980, Arleen Lorrance co–authored *The love project way* with Diane Kennedy Pike. Lorrance referred to a principle of "Be the change you want to see happen, instead of trying to change everyone else." Interestingly, Al Gore possibly used the "we must be the change we wish to see in the world" quote first, in his book *Earth in the balance* in 1992.
3. For an in–depth analysis of the rise of Hitler see; Shirer, W.L. 1993. *The Rise and Fall of the Third Reich*. London, England: Bison Books Ltd.
4. For one reference to the RBS small business scandal, see www.bbc.co.uk. 2016. "RBS Squeezed Struggling Businesses to Boost Profits, Leak Reveals,"

https://www.bbc.co.uk/news/uk-37591335, (accessed September 26, 2018).

5. Keltner, D. 2007. "The Power Paradox," *Greater Good Magazine*. https://greatergood.berkeley.edu/article/item/power_paradox, (accessed July 17, 2018).

6. Organizational Behavior. University of Minnesota. 2018. "The Power to Influence," http://open.lib.umn.edu/organizationalbehavior/chapter/13-3-the-power-to-influence/, (accessed July 18, 2018).

7. Covey, S.R. 1999. *The 7 Habits of Highly Effective People*. London, England: Simon & Schuster.

8. Simon, P., and A. Garfunkel. 1969. *The Boxer*. Nashville, TN: Columbia Records.

9. Rivera, D. 2010. "The Power to Define Reality: Whose Reality is Real?" *Psychology Today*. https://www.psychologytoday.com/gb/blog/microaggressions-in-everyday-life/201010/the-power-define-reality, (accessed July 18, 2018).

Chapter 12—The Clarion Call to Power

1. Monty Python. 1979. *The Life of Brian*. London, England: HandMade Films.

About the Author

Mark Eyre is the director of Brilliant Futures, specializing in helping business people to achieve their career and personal goals. An inspired coach, facilitator, and writer, his work spans leadership and career development, organization development, and employee well-being. He brings 30 years' experience of working in a variety of organizations, including universities, manufacturing, government, and financial services. Starting in human resources, his great passion was always in learning and personal development. He lives in Scotland, with his wife and two children. His spare-time interests are in the future of society, philosophy, and sport!

Index

OTHER TITLES IN OUR BUSINESS ETHICS AND CORPORATE CITIZENSHIP COLLECTION

David Wasieleski, *Editor*

- *Engaging Millennials for Ethical Leadership: What Works For Young Professionals and Their Managers* by Jessica McManus Warnell
- *Sales Ethics: How To Sell Effectively While Doing the Right Thing* by Alberto Aleo and Alice Alessandri
- *Working Ethically in Finance: Clarifying Our Vocation* by Anthony Asher
- *A Strategic and Tactical Approach to Global Business Ethics, Second Edition* by Lawrence A. Beer
- *Shaping the Future of Work: What Future Worker, Business, Government, and Education Leaders Need To Do For All To Prosper* by Thomas A. Kochan
- *War Stories: Fighting, Competing, Imagining, Leading* by Leigh Hafrey
- *Social Media Ethics Made Easy: How to Comply with FTC Guidelines* by Joseph W. Barnes
- *Adapting to Change: The Business of Climate Resilience* by Ann Goodman
- *Educating Business Professionals: The Call Beyond Competence and Expertise* by Lana S. Nino and Susan D. Gotsch

Announcing the Business Expert Press Digital Library

Concise e-books business students need for classroom and research

This book can also be purchased in an e-book collection by your library as

- *a one-time purchase,*
- *that is owned forever,*
- *allows for simultaneous readers,*
- *has no restrictions on printing, and*
- *can be downloaded as PDFs from within the library community.*

Our digital library collections are a great solution to beat the rising cost of textbooks. E-books can be loaded into their course management systems or onto student's e-book readers.

The **Business Expert Press** digital libraries are very affordable, with no obligation to buy in future years. For more information, please visit **www.businessexpertpress.com/librarians**. To set up a trial in the United States, please email **sales@businessexpertpress.com**.

www.ingramcontent.com/pod-product-compliance
Lightning Source LLC
Chambersburg PA
CBHW061214220326
41599CB00025B/4640